GODFIDENCE

A Grandfather's Legacy of Faith and Life
Stories that Proves God's Existence

Mark W. Bruton

Published by: Bruton's Publishing
First Edition: August 2024

Disclaimer

This is a work of nonfiction. The events depicted in this book are presented to the best of the author's memory and knowledge and verified by eyewitness accounts. The stories are true, and the places described are authentic. However, in some instances, names and identifying details have been changed to protect the privacy of individuals. While some characters have given permission to use their real names, others have not, and their names have been altered accordingly. Any resemblance to persons living or dead or to actual events beyond those described is purely coincidental.

Cover design by: Mark W. Bruton
Editing and Formatting: Turnedpagesco.com
Printed in the United States of America

For information about special discounts for bulk purchases, please contact [Bruton's Publishing].

Dedication

To ***Mai-Britt***, my beloved wife and true soulmate, your steady faith, boundless support, and enduring love have been my guiding lights. Thank you for standing by me through every trial and celebrating every victory. Your encouragement propelled me to complete this book, leaving a lasting legacy for our family.

To ***Isaac, Jacob, and Rebekah***, my cherished children, you embody God's blessings in my life. Your love and support have enriched my journey, teaching me the meaning of unconditional love and grace. This book is dedicated to you as a testament to our family's legacy of faith.

To ***Kasen, Jaycee, Trace, Lexee, Rogen, Chandler, and Liam,*** my precious grandchildren, may the stories within these pages ignite a flame of faith within your hearts, guiding you to trust our Heavenly Father's goodness.

Finally, to ***Monte Munkres,*** my lifelong friend, closer than a brother, your unwavering friendship has been my source of strength, laughter, and joy. This book is dedicated to our extraordinary forty-five-year friendship, a testament to the power of camaraderie and the example of a loyal companion.

Mai-Britt

My three children

Isaac Jacob Becky

My 7 Grandchildren

Monte Munkres- Best friend for 45 years

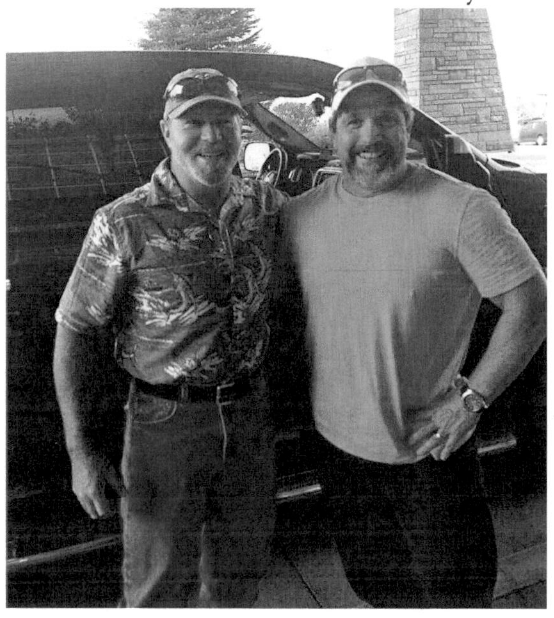

Table of Contents:

Introduction

A good man leaves an inheritance to his children's children.
Proverbs 13:22

Welcome to the Broken Halo club, my fellow stumblers, fumblers, and failures. If your feet trip over your shoelaces while trying to walk the straight and narrow, and if you find it difficult to position your halo over your horns, this book is for you.

However, if you are a super-Christian who never makes mistakes, this book is not for you.

If you have memorized half of the Bible and the rest in its original language and your steps never wander from the Lord's chosen path, you will not relate to this life story.

Do you belong to the sacred society for snubbing sinners? Are you a devout husband or wife who never argues or has thoughts that stray? Are you a parent who always does it right?

Friend, if you are consistent in living a godly and holy life, then with sincerity, I applaud and want to be like you. Respect is deserved.

This book comes with an honest disclaimer: It is intended for the Broken Halo club, not for those who have it all together.

It is crafted for the rest of us who strive earnestly but often fall short, making us feel as though God is displeased with us.

It is for those who are part saint and part rebel—we have made so many trips to hell and back that we have frequent flyer miles. We've got the best intentions, but we sometimes fumble the ball when we should be doing touchdown dances.

The words you are about to read are a spiritual labor of love, likened to the miracle of childbirth. Seeds sown in my heart long ago have grown into the precious baby now cradled in your hands.

In the pages ahead, each story is a mosaic, a vivid brushstroke on the canvas of my life, capturing moments of despair turning to hope, failure exchanged with forgiveness, adversity yielding to triumph, and brokenness being mended by a loving Creator.

Journeying through the corridors of time, you will experience the divine encounters that transformed my doubts into confident faith (Godfidence).

The term "Godfidence" was initially coined by Marshawn Evans Daniels. I am grateful that she inspired us with this word because I cannot find a better term to articulate the theme of this book.

"What is Godfidence?" you may ask. Simply put, confidence relies on our limited strength and ability, but Godfidence relies solely on God's unlimited power and His ability to change things in an instant.

Godfidence is trusting that all things, even complex and painful things, can work together for good if we tune into the Spirit who is at work in us.

In peeling back the layers of my experiences, you'll discover that God's goodness shines through even in the most unexpected places and at the darkest hours. These are not fanciful fables or embellished tales; they are genuine chronicles of a life touched by a Heavenly Father who weaves His grace into the fabric of our existence.

Let me clarify: This book is not about boasting of my accomplishments or powerful faith. Instead, it is an opportunity to witness a mighty and compassionate Heavenly Father whose presence is constant and whose power knows no bounds.

Consider this my "Bragimony". "What is a Bragimony?" one might ask. Soon, it will become apparent that the writer has nothing to brag about except his awesome God. Through the experiences shared in these chapters, the goal is to unveil the simple faith of an ordinary man in the presence of an extraordinary God.

He has walked with me through the highs and lows of life, guiding me through treacherous valleys and leading me to victorious mountaintops. He has been my refuge in times of despair, my healer in moments of sickness, my provider in seasons of lack, and the lifter of my head when I have failed.

Delving into this narrative, I will be candid and vulnerable at times, laying bare my failures and imperfections, and allowing you, dear reader, to witness the goodness of the Lord, even in the face of monumental missteps.

In those moments when I stumbled most, God still answered my prayers with divine precision, offered His glorious light to direct me when I strayed in darkness, and flung open doors of opportunity when I least deserved them.

May this book stand as a bridge—a conduit for the sacred legacy and rich heritage of unwavering faith. Those who harbor even a shadow of doubt regarding the Almighty's existence can rest assured that such skepticism will wither away upon encountering these vivid personal stories. To me, they are unassailable; for I have not only recounted them but also lived them.

The reader will discover that I have not attempted to impress anyone with eloquence or flamboyant words. Instead, I want to speak to your heart as though we are having a heartfelt conversation while sitting by a mountain stream or a campfire.

So, open the doors of your hearts, quicken your spirits, and come along on this exhilarating journey beside me. May these testimonies blaze like a lantern, casting a brilliant light on your path, leading you deeper into the presence of the One who beckons, "Ask, and you shall receive; seek, and you shall find" (Luke 11:9-10).

Before concluding this chapter, I want to share my recent experience with a discouraged friend. If you are like me, you will relate to his daily battle between good and evil.

Sitting across from my friend, I could detect the weight of spiritual combat etched on his face.

"Mark," he sighed, "I just can't manage to get it right. The power of sin within me keeps sabotaging my best intentions. The desire to do the right thing is present, but something within me always rebels."

Recognizing the familiar battle, I gave him an affirmative nod and said, "I understand what you mean. Your willpower is determined to do right, but you can't pull it off and end up doing wrong instead.

"The same struggle rages in me when I try to do the right thing," I explained with empathy. "My will to not sin is sincere, but then, I do it anyway." A part of me is downright rebellious, and when least expected, the scoundrel takes charge."

He gazed at me with relief in his eyes. "Exactly! Knowing I have someone who relates to my struggles is encouraging. Mark, why don't my well-meaning decisions translate into actions? Something has gone wrong deep within me, and it gets the better of me every time."

We shared a moment of silent acknowledgment as we grappled with the paradox of our virtuous intentions and repeated failures.

"The moment I decide to do good," my friend confessed, "sin is immediately present to trip me up, a constant daily battle."

He let out a deep sigh, a mix of frustration and acceptance. "Brother, I need help. Something more than my willpower is needed to conquer this cycle that I can't seem to break."

Observing the pain of his dilemma, a revelation dawned. "You know, you are not alone. This is a daily battle we all face, but there is hope. We are in this together, and there is a way out of this cycle."

Oh, did I mention that my friend's name was Paul, and these were the very words he echoed in Romans 7:17-23 (MSG)?

That's right! This struggle between right and wrong was once penned by the Apostle Paul himself, who would go on to shape the

Christian faith, plant hundreds of churches, and write two-thirds of the New Testament despite his struggles with the sinful nature.

Friend, you, too, are not alone. There is a way to break free of this up-and-down moral treadmill (Roller Coaster Christianity).

Therefore, the following pages aim to share, chapter by chapter, how many, including myself, have learned to tame the beast that resides in all of us and embrace the finished work of Christ, enabling us to enjoy the life Jesus died to give us.

Here is a comforting thought: When God calls you to His service, He already factors in your stupidity. Jesus knew what He was getting when He died for you. He loves you just as you are, but He values you too much to leave you that way.

As we begin this daring faith-filled pilgrimage, brace yourself to witness the breathtaking marvels of a Heavenly Father who yearns to reveal Himself to you. Remember, the scriptures declare, "The Lord longs to be gracious to you" (Isaiah 30:18).

The Bible verses that inspired me to write this book are on the Divine Whispers page. These verses were the seeds of divine inspiration and the foundation for this humble work.

For many years, I have read these inspired words and heard the still, small voice of the Holy Spirit whispering to me, "Son, I want you to write about your story—the story of how God has been so good to you and accomplished so many miraculous things throughout your life. It will be a legacy to bolster the faith of your children and grandchildren and strengthen the faith of many who struggle through the ups and downs of this life."

Therefore, out of obedience to God, I present this book with deep reverence and offer you the countless divine encounters that sculpted my unshakeable "Godfidence."

[1]

[1] Tool, D. E. (2024). *Good Versus Evil* [Digital image]. Online. https://chatgpt.com/c/5f5217cb-e104-4e80-82b0-8c842be4e86a

Divine Whispers

Through the verses that inspired these pages, may you be uplifted, encouraged, and reminded of the countless ways God has consistently blessed, protected, and provided for you. Johnson Oatman wrote the old song, ***"Count your many blessings, name them one by one, Count your many blessings and see what God has done."*** [2] May this journey into the realm of gratitude and worship ignite a fire of thanksgiving within your soul, causing you to magnify the Lord for His never-ending love and faithful provision. May it cause you to see God's goodness in everything, good and bad, on the mountaintops and valleys. These verses were the seeds of divine inspiration and the foundation for this book:

Psalm 9:1 NIV
"I will give thanks to the LORD with my whole heart;
I will recount all of your wonderful deeds".

Psalm 26: 7 NLT
… I come to your altar, O LORD,
proclaiming thanksgiving aloud,
and telling all your wondrous deeds.

Proverbs 3: 5-6 NLT
5. Trust in the Lord with all your heart;
do not depend on your own understanding.
6. Seek his will in all you do,
and he will show you which path to take. (Emphasis mine)

---

[2] Oatman, J. (n.d.). *Count Your Blessings*. Timeless Truths- Free Online Library. Retrieved June 23, 2023, from https://library.timelesstruths.org/music/Count_Your_Blessings/

Psalm 77: 11-12 NLT
11. But then I recall all you have done, O Lord;
I remember your wonderful deeds of long ago.
12. They are constantly in my thoughts.

Psalm 78: 4 NLT
4. We will not hide these truths from our children;
we will tell the next generation
about the glorious deeds of the Lord,
about his power and his mighty wonders.

Psalm 103: 2-5 NLT
2. Let all that I am praise the Lord;
may I never forget the good things he does for me.
3. He forgives all my sins
and heals all my diseases.
4. He redeems me from death
and crowns me with love and tender mercies.
5. He fills my life with good things.
My youth is renewed like the eagle's!

Psalms 105: 1-5 NLT
1. Give thanks to the Lord and proclaim his greatness.
Let the whole world know what he has done.
2. Sing to him; yes, sing his praises.
Tell everyone about his wonderful deeds.
3. Exult in his holy name;
rejoice, you who worship the Lord.
4. Search for the Lord and for his strength;
continually seek him.
5. Remember the wonders he has performed,
his miracles, and the rulings he has given.

Psalm 106: 1-2 NLT

1. Praise the Lord!
Give thanks to the Lord, for he is good!
His faithful love endures forever.
2. Who can list the glorious miracles of the Lord?
Who can ever praise him enough?

Psalm 106: 6-7 NLT

6. Like our ancestors, we have sinned.
We have done wrong! We have acted wickedly!
7. Our ancestors in Egypt were not impressed by the Lord's miraculous deeds. They soon forgot his many acts of kindness to them.
Instead, they rebelled against him at the Red Sea.

Psalm 107:6-9 NLT

6. "Lord, help!" they cried in their trouble,
and he rescued them from their distress.
7. He led them straight to safety,
to a city where they could live.
8. Let them praise the Lord for his great love
and for the wonderful things he has done for them.
9. For he satisfies the thirsty and fills the hungry with good things.

Psalm 107: 14-15 NLT

14. He led them from the darkness and deepest gloom;
he snapped their chains.
15. Let them praise the Lord for his great love
and for the wonderful things he has done for them.

Psalm 107:21-22 NLT
21. Let them praise the Lord for his great love
and for the wonderful things he has done for them.
22. Let them offer sacrifices of thanksgiving
and sing joyfully about his glorious acts.

Psalm 107:43 NLT
43. Those who are wise will take all this to heart;
they will see in our history the faithful love of the Lord.

Psalm 111: 1-4 NLT
1. 'Praise the Lord!
I will thank the Lord with all my heart
as I meet with his godly people.
2. How amazing are the deeds of the Lord!
All who delight in him should ponder them.
3. Everything he does reveals his glory and majesty.
His righteousness never fails.
4. He causes us to remember his wonderful works.
How gracious and merciful is our Lord!

Psalm 118: 14-17 NLT
14. The Lord is my strength and my song; he has given me victory.
15. Songs of joy and victory are sung in the camp of the godly.
The strong right arm of the Lord has done glorious things!
16. The strong right arm of the Lord is raised in triumph.
The strong right arm of the Lord has done glorious things!
17. I will not die; instead, I will live to tell what the Lord has done.

Joshua 1: 8-9 NLT

8. Study this Book of Instruction continually. Meditate on it day and night
so you will be sure to obey everything written in it. Only then will you prosper
and succeed in all you do.
9. This is my command—be strong and courageous! Do not be afraid or discouraged. For the Lord, your God is with you wherever you go."

The Seeds of Faith Come from the Word of God.[3]

[3] Tool, D. T. (2024). *Open Bible radiating light* [Photograph]. Online. https://chatgpt.com/c/bec1e8aa-0a5c-4a6b-954c-dda331a0abcd

PART 1

Painful Beginnings

1

Seeds of Faith

Painful Beginnings

The sun began its descent, painting the sky in gold, orange, and pink hues when an older man stumbled upon a wounded sparrow. Its tiny heart thumped under feathered warmth, as its wing fluttered weakly against his palm. The man pulled out a bandage from his pocket and wrapped the fragile wing with gentleness, his voice deep, softening to a tender murmur as he spoke to the little bird.

"There, there, little one," he said with a gentle and soothing voice. "You're safe now. No need to be afraid."

Still wide and frantic, the sparrow's eyes began to calm as it listened to the old man's peaceful rhythm.

"Imagine the vast, open skies," the man continued in a warm tone. "Feel the wind beneath your wings, lifting you high above the treetops."

The bird's heartbeat, fluttering like a trapped butterfly, soon steadied.

"You'll fly again, I promise," he whispered, securing the bandage. "You will soar with grace and freedom, just like you are meant to."

The bird's tiny body quivered, but there was a newfound stillness, a sense of trust in the man's comforting presence.

"You have a fierce spirit, little one," the man said, a smile touching his lips.

"I see it in your eyes. You remind me of someone with resilience who overcame the odds in his life."

The sparrow seemed to relax even more, its frantic eyes now watching the man with curiosity and calm.

"We all face challenges," he continued, his voice a soothing balm. "But we endure, heal, and find our strength again. Just like you will."

He finished wrapping the wing and stroked the little critter's head with a finger.

"There you go, all set," he said. "Rest now. Dream of the skies and the freedom of flight. Your time will come again."

The sparrow's eyes closed, its body nestling into the man's hand, comforted by the promise of healing and the gentle touch of its caregiver.

The tiny bird mirrored the tales of resilience and redemption the man carried in his own soul. Their bond grew, and each found solace and strength in the other's presence.

The man continued to tend to his wee, little friend, as his mind began to wander back to the early years of his life when his family home failed to provide sanctuary. The oppressive fear that had once gripped his soul haunted him since he was only six years old.

In these moments of reflection, the man recognized an emotional parallel between his life and the sparrow's plight—both fragile, yearning for freedom and healing, and both in the hands of a merciful caregiver. His thoughts drifted back to those trials that shaped him:

The apartment seemed colder than usual that night as if the walls had braced themselves for the impending storm. A young boy sat in the dark living room, the flickering lamp in the corner casting shadows that danced with the air's tension. The place exuded coldness, not in temperature but in the atmosphere that filled it—a mixture of fear and apprehension. The boy's mother paced back and forth, her hands wringing together as if trying to squeeze out the courage to face what she was about to do.

This scene set the stage for a trial not held in any courtroom but in the heart and life of a young boy who could anticipate what was coming even before his mother spoke. The silence thickened, charged with an unspoken understanding of her decision. This choice would once again alter the course of their lives.

"Momma, please," the boy's voice broke through the stillness, a mix of desperation and fear.

"Don't go back to him! That monster hasn't changed. He will never change." The boy's words, though trembling, carried the weight of courage and determination that belied his young age.

The mother's face became a battlefield of emotions, torn between the love for her son and the misplaced hope in a man who had brought them nothing but pain.

"But he's different now," she whispered, more to herself than her son. "I believe him because he promised."

"Mom, how can you believe him after everything he has done to us? How can we go back into that dark hell?" The boy's voice trembled, not from the cold but from the sheer terror at the thought of returning to the man who had made their lives a never-ending nightmare.

The small but defiant youngster stood before the door as if his slender frame could somehow block the path to their impending doom. His eyes, full of fear, also burned with a determination that belied his years. The mother's shoulders slumped, her eyes averted from his gaze, already resigned to her decision. This trial would test the boy beyond his years—a journey that would take him through the darkest valleys but also to the highest peaks of the human spirit.

The boy's grandmother became his rock during these tumultuous times. She provided warmth in the cold and light in the darkness. She nurtured his curious mind, not just with words, but with actions. Bouncing him on her knee as she read Bible stories in picture books, she planted seeds of hope and faith in his young heart. The scent of fresh-baked bread and apple pie always filled her kitchen, a stark contrast to the tense atmosphere of his mother's apartment. Sunlight and fresh air danced through the curtains, a reminder of the world outside—a world full of possibilities and God's love.

The boy's stepfather ruled over their home like a menacing monster, his very presence a tangible force of terror. Each day, the man's eyes burned with unpredictable rage—his fists clenched, and his voice a low, simmering growl that could erupt into a violent storm without warning. Every night brought confrontations that echoed through the walls, the sounds of shouting and breaking objects becoming a twisted lullaby.

The youngster's heart pounded with dread whenever the clock inched toward 3:00 PM, the end of school signaling the beginning of another night in the dragon's lair.

Fear gripped him so tight that he found himself wetting his pants daily, the terror of facing his stepfather's wrath too much to contain. The walk home each day was a march toward an expected peril, each step heavier than the last. This torment continued for years, the boy's innocence eroding with each passing day. Yet, he endured, his spirit unbroken.

At nine years old, a heartbreaking decision confronted him. The lad would plead with his mother to choose between him and the cruel, abusive man. The mother's eyes were vacant, and her voice resigned; she chose the abusive man over her own son. Crushed but resolute, the young lad packed his belongings and left to live with his father in another town, seeking refuge from the constant nightmare that had consumed his young life. His decision, though heartbreaking, was a testament to his strength and independence.

The young man idolized his dad, a man of velvet and steel, strength and kindness—a stark contrast to the sinister stepfather. Their bond was forged through shared experiences in the great outdoors—hunting, fishing, camping—and these moments provided a respite for the boy and a glimpse into a different life filled with love and respect.

Five years later, the boy's darkest night descended without warning. Fourteen and just beginning his ninth-grade year of high school, he found himself thrust into a turbulence of grief again. The once-familiar corridors of his school twisted into an alien labyrinth, the sterile walls, and buzzing fluorescent lights a harsh contrast to the chaos churning inside him.

As his brother and sister delivered the devastating news of their mother's death, the boy's vision wavered, and the world around him faded into a blur. His legs were heavy, and a cold numbness spread through his body as if the ground had been yanked from beneath his feet, leaving him suspended in a void of sorrow and disbelief.

Every breath came shallow and shaky, the weight of his loss pressing down on his chest like an iron vise, squeezing out the last bits of his childhood innocence.

His grief was compounded when a family member accused him saying, "If you had been there, this would never have happened; it's all your fault!" This accusation cut like a knife through his heart, adding guilt to the crushing weight of this tragedy.

Amidst his internal turmoil at the graveside service, he found a moment of peace before a massive statue of Jesus with His arms outstretched. In his deepest despair, it was here that he first sensed the touch of divine comfort, a warmth that enveloped him, offering a glimmer of hope in the darkness.

This event did not mark the end of his trials but rather the beginning of his faith journey. Through rejection and bereavement, he found strength and purpose. The young man dedicated his life to helping others, using his experiences to guide those who faced their own darkness.

The climactic pinnacle of his journey tested his trust and resolve, pushing him to the limits of his endurance. Faced with the choice of letting life's circumstances make him bitter or better, he chose the latter by forgiving the man who killed his mother.

This choice strengthened him, solidified his trust in the Lord, and made him a testament to the power of God's love and the resilience of the human spirit.

The narrative comes full circle. The boy, now a man, reflects on his journey, a living example of healing, resilience, and the transformative power of love.

In full disclosure, I am that boy. The story above is my narrative of overcoming the darkest nights to find the dawn of a new day.

I share my difficult experiences to illustrate how God introduced His compassionate care and presence in my life, much like the tale of the sparrow who learned to fly again through healing and a gentle touch. Like the wounded bird, I was cared for, and my wings mended, allowing me to soar into the light of a new beginning.

These events merely planted the seeds of my faith. The following chapters unveil how those seeds grew and came to life—a faith adventure! Buckle up; it's quite a ride![4]

[4] Tool, D. E. (2024). Young Mark, defending His Mother [Digital depiction]. Online.OpenAI. (2024). ChatGPT (4o) [Large language model]. https://chatgpt.com/c/67956650-b0da-4db0-a561-08825e073d46

Takeaways and Lessons Learned:

1. **Resilience in the Face of Adversity:** The chapter illustrates the power of resilience through personal challenges. The author's journey from a traumatic childhood to a place of healing and strength is a testament to the human spirit's capacity to endure and thrive despite adversity.

2. **The Healing Power of Compassion:** The narrative highlights how acts of kindness and compassion can significantly impact both the giver and the receiver. The man's care for the wounded sparrow mirrors the compassionate support he received from the Lord and others throughout his life, demonstrating how empathy and love can lead to profound healing.

3. **Transformation Through Faith:** The author's story emphasizes the transformative power of faith. By trusting in God's plan and finding strength in divine guidance, the author could overcome significant challenges, forgive those who wronged him, and ultimately find a sense of purpose and peace.

Reflection Questions for Application

1. **How Have I Demonstrated Resilience in My Life?**
   - Reflect on your challenges and how you responded to them. What personal strengths did you draw upon to overcome these difficulties? Consider how your experiences have shaped your resilience and what lessons you can apply to current or future challenges.

2. **In What Ways Can I Show Compassion to Others?**
   - Think about opportunities in your life to offer kindness and support to those in need. How can you be a source of comfort

and healing for others, just as the man was for the wounded sparrow? Reflect on the impact of your compassionate actions on yourself and those you help.

3. **How Has My Faith Guided Me Through Difficult Times?**
   - Consider the role of faith in your life, especially during periods of hardship. How has your belief system provided strength, comfort, and direction when facing challenges? Reflect on how your faith journey has evolved and how you can continue to nurture and rely on it, moving forward.

2

From LOST To Found

The Tug Of Grace

1980 marked a pivotal juncture in my life—a year of transformation that would forever alter the course of my journey. The downward spiral of my emotional state had commenced following the loss of my grandpa and mother in 1976. In the wake of this profound grief, an angry chip had settled on my shoulder, an ever-present companion.

This anger found an outlet in combat sports like wrestling and American football, earning me the reputation of being a brawler and a street fighter. Initiating fights was not my usual practice, but I was quick to engage in them if necessary. To my chagrin, I became proficient. For example, if a bully targeted a disabled kid, I would be on him like gummy bears on a set of braces. Despite the nobility of my actions, I always carried a sense of post-brawl shame.

My mastery in concealing years of pent-up anger and hatred led to these occasional brawls becoming my release valve. Despite how close I came on several occasions, it's a wonder I never faced jail time for my ornery deeds—the consequences I deserve. Countless hours were devoted to gaining size and strength in the weight room and on the wrestling mat. "Why?" one might ask. It is because I was preparing for only one thing: retribution against the men who had abused my mother and me.

The plan was to track down those two tormentors and exact a devastating revenge. Vowing that when I got done with them, they would have to be wheeled into surgery on six separate tables, and their families could visit them at the hospital in rooms 340, 341, 342, 343, and 344. That was my plan! The Lord would present another path for my life, however.

The Lord was working behind the scenes, tugging at my heartstrings, and inviting me to come to Him and lay down my anger, hatred, and bitterness. The Lord planned to exchange these tumultuous emotions for peace, to replace hate with love, and to transform offense into forgiveness.

However, my spirit had become as hard as Chinese algebra, enclosed by an impenetrable shell, resistant to change. Blaise Pascal's words resonated with me: "There is a God-shaped vacuum in the heart of every man which cannot be satisfied by any created thing, but only by God, the Creator, made known through Jesus Christ." In 1980, my soul felt that emptiness deep inside. On the surface, my life appeared happy and successful. Due to my vitality and cheerful personality, I gained popularity in high school. My friends called me a human "Tigger," like the character from Winnie the Pooh.

Being a dedicated athlete, I steered clear of harmful drugs but did indulge in a few pints of the barley buddy during the off-season. Despite this facade of happiness, the inner void grew more pronounced each day. Three months passed, and the Holy Spirit tugged at my heart more and more every day, calling me to higher ground. The precious Lord Jesus whispered to my empty heart, pulling at my soul like never before.

Many people find their way to Christ through a pastor's sermon, an evangelist, or a friend's witness. My path was different. The Heavenly Father dealt with me on a personal level, much like the Apostle Paul on the road to Damascus. Thanks to early childhood experiences, I had never doubted God's existence, but the seeds of salvation were now ripe for the harvest.

In 1980, I worked for my girlfriend's father, who owned a log and firewood business. The job proved grueling and demanding, but God placed me in that position with a divine purpose. Mr. Dale Huff was a rugged, robust, tenacious individual with a unique sense of humor. Dale exemplified authentic masculinity. Working alongside him was a blessing and a trial. Dale's mentorship taught me how to work as a man should, and I discovered humility in the process.

We ventured to the mountains each day before dawn to begin our strenuous toil. Dale's coffee was strong enough to kill Blackwater fever, but it prepared us for the day ahead. Sharpening saws, cutting trees, and loading them onto trucks proved a relentless challenge, but it instilled endurance within me. The grueling labor, day in and day out, developed my physical stamina. After a summer of such exertion, I developed the strength of Sisyphus pushing that massive stone up the eternal hill. Throwing lumber in and out of the truck all day was demanding on the body. Returning home each day, I felt like a test dummy for an ejection seat on a helicopter.

Weeks passed, and I grappled with severe depression. The world seemed drained of color, the sky devoid of its usual blue, and the birds ceased to sing. Then came the morning that would change my life forever.

I was splitting logs on Mr. Huff's custom wood splitter, a machine monster capable of slicing through logs faster than you can say, "Timmy fell in the well!" The weight of the world pressed down on my shoulders on this particular day, and I sat on a pile of timber and sobbed. My prayer, spoken through tears, was filled with desperation: "Lord, I know you are there, although we haven't talked in a long time. To show that You still care about me, please help me. Please reveal to me a sign that You are still here, taking an interest in my life and my future. My heart aches, and I don't know what to do. Please assure me that everything will be okay."

What happened next defies explanation. It was as if Heaven itself descended, enveloping me in a blanket of love and a sense of peace that surpassed all understanding. There had never been a time when I experienced such tranquillity, and I cried tears of joy from the depths of my soul. The sky appeared bluer than ever, the birds sang melodies sweeter than a symphony, and the world regained its vibrant colors, and I felt like a million pounds had been lifted from my shoulders. The Gentle Shepherd had embraced me as He whispered the comforting words of my earthly father: "Mark B., everything will be alright; Ole Dad is right here."

The Lord had answered my prayer in an intense, personal way, but this was only the beginning, the catalyst for my quest to discover my purpose.

After this event, I began to attend church every Sunday. I sensed the Holy Spirit nudging me toward surrender. The Holy Spirit had been beckoning me for three months, prompting me to respond to His call. Resistance was my response, as I feared He would transform me into a preacher or a missionary, forced to live on bugs and worms in some remote corner of the earth.

The Lord was unrelenting because He knew how much I needed Him and had an extraordinary plan for my life: (Jeremiah 29:11 NLT) "For I know the plans I have for you, says the Lord. They are plans for good and not for disaster, to give you a future and a hope."

In August of that year, a traveling evangelist named Forrest T. Jackson arrived to hold revival meetings for a week. His messages were power-packed and magnetic in their delivery, and I attended every night, but my grip on the pew remained steadfast. Everything changed at the First Baptist Church in Delta, Colorado, one fateful morning.

After the preacher concluded his sermon, he invited those who desired to dedicate their lives to Christ to come forward.

The congregation began to sing the hymn, "The Savior is Waiting." An extraordinary thing happened as I clung to the oak bench with all my might. The minister halted the song with a firm resolve and addressed the congregation: "Ladies and gentlemen, I have never done this in my forty years of evangelism; the Holy Spirit is telling me that someone here needs to heed the words of this song.

The Father above is calling you to follow Him today. Please, do not delay another day! Let us sing one more stanza of the hymn. You must come if you are the one He is speaking to." The folks resumed singing, and I read the words with deep introspection.

The Savior's Call

The Savior is waiting to enter your heart;
Why don't you let Him come in?
There is nothing in this world to keep you apart;
What is your answer to Him?
Time after time, He has waited before,
And now He is waiting again
To see if you are willing to open the door;
Oh, how He wants to come in.
If you take one step toward the Savior, my friend,
You will find His arms open wide.
Receive Him, and all of your darkness will end;
Within your heart, He will abide. [5]

The heartfelt words filled the air as the minister leaned closer to the microphone while we sang, his voice charged with earnestness. "Friend, have you felt the gentle tug of the Holy Spirit who loves you, only to resist it? Today, He is calling you. Please, don't delay; seize this opportunity!"

In that decisive moment, a now-or-never crossroad emerged. Jesus finally conquered my heart, and I released my firm grip on the pew, marking the beginning of a life-changing journey down the

[5] Carmichael, R. (1958). The Savior is Waiting (p. online). https://thescottspot.wordpress.com/2016/09/21/the-savior-is-waiting-written-in-1958/

aisle—a public declaration of surrender to Christ. Not a single dry eye remained in the entire building.

The Pastor bowed his head in prayer with me. After he uttered the final Amen, I glanced up to find the whole Bruton family standing behind me; the approving smiles of my kin radiated warmth. This support held incredible significance, as our history had been marked by discord and estrangement.

Years of alienation had cast me as the family's black sheep, but it was evident that the Heavenly Father was in the process of restoring the shattered fragments of my life. This moment began a new chapter that would unfold with joy and pain.

The storms on the horizon loomed, but with the Lord's help, I knew I could weather them all. Looking back, I shudder to think how I might have faced the trials ahead without Him by my side. Thank you, Lord, for rescuing my soul and etching my name into the Lamb's Book of Life. The words to the old hymn, "Amazing Grace," echoed in my mind: "I once was lost, but now I am found..."

In the following chapters, you will witness the remarkable way God manifested Himself in my life and became real to me. Hold tight; this adventure promises to be exhilarating.

Digital depiction of my final surrender

Digital depiction of my final surrender [6]

Takeaways and Lessons Learned:

1. **The Transformative Power of Faith:** The chapter highlights how a personal encounter with faith can lead to profound transformation. The author's journey from anger and bitterness to peace and purpose underscores the power of faith to heal and redirect one's life.

2. **The Importance of Surrender:** The narrative emphasizes the significance of surrendering to Jesus Christ for salvation. The author's initial resistance and eventual submission to God's call demonstrate that actual change often requires letting go of control and trusting in a greater plan.
3. **The Role of Community and Support:** The chapter illustrates the vital role of community and support in one's

[6] Tool, D. E. (2024). Final Surrender [Digital image]. Online. Tool, D. E. (2024). Young Man Asking God for Help [Digital image]. Online. OpenAI. (2024). ChatGPT (4o) [Large language model]. https://chatgpt.com/c/67956650-b0da-4db0-a561-08825e073d46

faith journey. The author's family's acceptance and encouragement from mentors and church members played a crucial part in his spiritual growth and healing.

Reflection Questions for Application:

1. **How Has My Faith Transformed My Life?:** Reflect on moments when your faith has led to significant changes in your life. How did these experiences shape your perspective, behavior, and sense of purpose? Consider the ways faith has guided you through difficult times and brought you peace.

2. **What Areas of My Life Do I Need to Surrender?:** Think about aspects of your life where you might be holding on too tightly. What fears or uncertainties prevent you from fully trusting in God? Reflect on how surrendering these areas could lead to greater peace and transformation.

3. **How Can I Support Others on Their Faith Journey?:** Consider how you can be a source of encouragement and support for others in their spiritual journeys. Reflect on the impact that a supportive community has had on your own faith development, and think about ways you can extend that same support to those around you.

3

When Baptism Goes Awry:

Slippery Steps and a Drowned Pastor

It has often been said of me, "If there's a hard way to do something, Bruton will find it every time. If anything can go wrong, it will happen to him." I wish I could disagree with that statement, but it is true. My reputation for calamity has provided countless laughs for many people.

Take, for instance, my ill-fated attempt to show off my cliff-diving skills to a group of youngsters. A swan dive from thirty feet turned into a perfect belly flop, giving me the appearance of a boiled lobster and nearly paralyzing me. Or the time I tested a new bike in the store, ending in a spectacular crash. And who could forget the bicycle handstand sidewalk faceplant? What about the over-tightened toe clips that sent me sprawling into a busy intersection, dragging my bike out of the street while still stuck in the clips? The tales are endless.

If you had a few days, my wife and family would gladly regale you with more stories while tears of laughter stream down their cheeks. Although I'm happy to bring such joy into their lives, I bear the scars of those countless mishaps.

The story I'm about to tell will undoubtedly amuse you. However, it is one of my life's most embarrassing moments. When I first recounted this tale to my family, they looked at each other and said in unison, "Of course!" With their heads thrown back, and loud laughter and tears followed.

Setting the Scene

Before I reveal this hilarious incident, let me explain why I felt compelled to be baptized. After surrendering my life to Jesus, I learned it was essential to make a public declaration through baptism. Baptism by immersion symbolizes a believer's identification with Christ's death, burial, and resurrection. It signifies the convert's acknowledgment that the old self has died with Christ and represents a new life in Him.

While different Christian traditions have varying views on baptism, it's important to note that baptism is not a requirement for salvation. As the Apostle Paul states in Ephesians 2:8-9, "For it is by grace you have been saved, through faith—and this is not from yourselves, it is the gift of God—not by works so that no one can boast." Baptism is a symbol of faith, not a prerequisite for entry into Heaven.

Now, let me set the scene for you. Picture a large, old-fashioned sanctuary filled with people. The baptismal was built into the wall behind the pastor's pulpit, with a large glass front so that the congregation could see the submerged person. The choir, adorned in beautiful burgundy-colored robes, sat below this window, often getting a few drops of water during baptisms.

On this particular Sunday, eleven of us were being baptized. The entire Bruton family filled the pews in their Sunday best. Grandma Bruton, the family matriarch, sat with all the regality of the Queen of England. My Uncle, Bob, with his rugged and stern look, was there too. My dad sat tall with all the pride of a Caesar. My brother and sister were present, excited to see this significant moment.

The Baptismal Service

After the morning sermon, the highly anticipated baptismal service began. With so many of us being baptized, I offered to assist others in and out of the baptismal tub. I noticed water building up on the stairs, making them slippery. An elderly lady began to slip, but I helped her as she entered and exited.

I waited to go last. When it was my turn to descend the daunting, slippery stairs, no one was around to help me. They were all in the back, taking off their wet robes. I thought, "It's me; what can go wrong?" Then I remembered all the times in my life when I was as clumsy as a one-legged spider. But not this time! This ceremony was too important and meaningful. Everything would be fine.

As I began my careful descent, the happy choir peered through the glass window, cheerfully watching. I wanted to stand tall and proud, as my family would expect. Then it happened!

In a split second, my feet slipped and spun like Wiley E. Coyote running at full speed. It happened so fast that I could do nothing to stop it. You guessed it. I did a full gainer–half–twist cannonball into the baptismal tank, missing the last four steps. Bless their hearts; the choir got hit with a two-foot wall of water. Seven took the brunt of it, looking like drowned rats in choir robes.

I took poor old Reverend Spindler down to the bottom with me. He gasped, choked, and spit when he emerged from the water. His glasses sat askew on the end of his nose. Mortified, I glanced at the congregation. The Bruton family had their heads hung down, rubbing their brows in embarrassment, but not my dad. He broke the uncomfortable silence with a loud yell, "That's MY boy!" The crowd erupted into knee-slap laughter.

Dear old Pastor Spindler straightened his glasses and addressed the congregation. "Well, folks," he said, "This is the first time in forty years of ministry that I have been baptized with the new convert. The Lord has His hands full with this one!" The crowd erupted into foot-stomping laughter again.

I've never heard the end of it. A plaque on that church wall should read, "Mark Bruton—the most comical baptism of all time." I trust my explanation of the meaning and importance of baptism was helpful. As for the story of my baptism, I hope it made you smile. It was a comical mishap that I will never forget, but it also reminds me that God's grace is always present, even in our mistakes and embarrassing moments.

Oh! And I'm pretty sure I heard God chuckle when this happened; and like my dad, I think He yelled across Heaven, "That's MY Boy!"

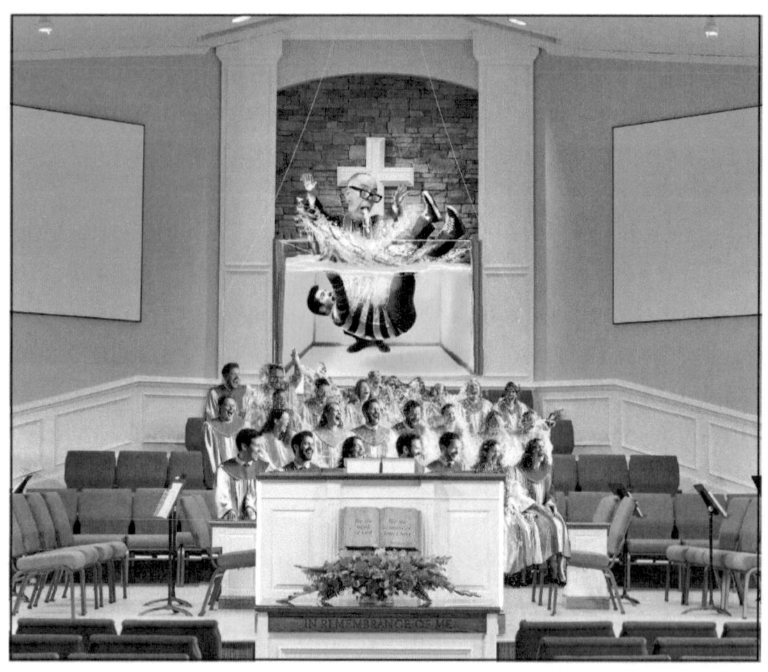

[7]

Digital depiction

[7] Bruton, M. W., Tool, D. E. (2024). When Baptism Goes Awry [Digital Art]. Online. OpenAI. (2024). [Large language model]. https://chatgpt.com/c/67956650-b0da-4db0-a561-08825e073d46

Takeaways and Lessons Learned:

- **Embracing Imperfection in Faith**: This chapter illustrates that our faith journey is not about being perfect but about embracing and learning from our imperfections. The author's humorous mishap during baptism shows that God's grace and love are ever-present, even in our clumsy and embarrassing moments.
- **Public Declaration of Faith**: Baptism is an important public declaration of one's faith in Jesus Christ. The author emphasizes its significance as a symbol of identification with Christ's death, burial, and resurrection, marking the beginning of a new life in Him.
- **Finding Joy in the Journey**: The author's ability to laugh at himself and find joy in his misadventures highlights the importance of maintaining a positive outlook and sense of humor, even when things don't go as planned. This perspective can transform potentially embarrassing moments into cherished memories.

Reflection Questions for Application

1. **How Do I Respond to Imperfections in My Faith Journey?**
   - Reflect on how you handle your own imperfections and mistakes in your faith journey. Do you tend to be overly critical of yourself, or can you find grace and humor in those moments? Consider how embracing imperfection can deepen your relationship with God and others.
2. **What Does the Public Declaration of Faith Mean to Me?**
   - Think about the ways you publicly declare your faith. Have you experienced moments when your faith was tested in public? How did you respond? Reflect on the

importance of these declarations and how they impact your spiritual growth and witness to others.

3. **How Can I Cultivate Joy and Humor in My Life?**
   - Consider the role of joy and humor in your life, especially during challenging or embarrassing situations. How can you develop a habit of finding the lighter side of life's mishaps? Reflect on how maintaining a positive outlook can enhance your overall well-being and relationship.

PART 2

When God Becomes Real

4

Divine Light for Dark Days

Learning to Navigate Loss

At first glance at this chapter's title, you might anticipate a sad and depressing explanation of the losses I've experienced in my life, but let me assure you, this chapter has a different purpose altogether. It does not seek sympathy or aim to foster discouragement. Instead, as you immerse yourself in these pages, you will witness a profound turning point that forever altered my life—and it can do the same for you. I intend to unveil how my encounter with the Almighty God became an undeniable and tangible reality amidst this loss. In short, God became real to me.

Through heartfelt anecdotes and moments of vulnerability, I will illustrate how God's soothing presence enveloped the ache within my heart. These recollections testify to His unwavering love, faithfulness, and existence, especially during life's darkest hours. Within the confines of this chapter, you will witness the extraordinary interplay between human affection and divine solace. Furthermore, you will uncover the transformative healing that comes to us when we surrender our pain into the compassionate arms of Jesus.

While I recount the myriad ways in which my Heavenly Father guided me through the darkest days of my life, I am reminded of the fitting words penned by Andraé Crouch:

"I've had many tears and sorrows,
and I've had questions for tomorrow;
there have been times I didn't know right from wrong.
But in every situation, God gave me blessed consolation
that my trials come only to make me strong.
Through it all, I've learned to trust in Jesus;
I've learned to trust in God. Through it all, through it all,
I've learned to depend upon His Word." [8]

Before we begin, I invite you to experience the beautiful relationship I shared with my dad, a bond that transcended father and son, making us best friends. Discover the essence of this remarkable man, a true man's man who epitomized hard work and determination. With his quick wit, sharp intelligence, and infectious laughter, my dad illuminated every moment we spent together as we created treasured memories that would shape my life forever.

From thrilling hunting adventures to scenic camping trips, fishing excursions on tranquil lakes, and even the thrill of sitting on his lap as I helped him steer a gigantic, big-rig semi-truck, we shared countless adventures that bonded us. However, as fate would have it, 1982 brought the most acute loss of my life—my beloved dad's sudden, untimely death. I was only nineteen years old, in my sophomore year of college, and it was in the face of overwhelming grief that God revealed Himself to me, making Him as real as the heart that beat in my chest. Let me elaborate.

The University I attended was just a quick forty-five-minute drive from my hometown, making it easy to head home on weekends to spend quality time with my pops. On that memorable Sunday, March

[8] Crouch, A. (n.d.). Through it All. Zion Lyrics. Retrieved February 25, 2023, from https://zionlyrics.com/lyrics/andrae-crouch-through-it-all-ive-learned-to-trust-in-jesus-lyricsae

13, 1982, the weekend routine was as usual: it was time for me to leave, my dad and I exchanged farewells, and I headed toward my car. Then, a surprising twist occurred. Upon departure, I glanced over my shoulder and saw my dad standing in the doorway, beckoning me back. It struck me as being odd because my dad had never done this before. So, I assumed I had forgotten something important. Curious, I retraced my steps inside. My dad gazed straight into my eyes; his words were sincere. "Mark B.," he said, "I want you to understand that no father in the history of time has ever been prouder of their child than I am of you. I love you, Son!"

I was so touched that I returned a comment in kind, saying, "Dad, there has never been a child in the history of time that was prouder to be a man's son than I am to be yours; I love you, Dad!" We embraced as tears of sincerity flowed down our cheeks. It was tough to leave after this tender moment. However, I had to return to start classes on Monday. As I left town, I had an extraordinary feeling, an acute realization that this would be the last time I would see my father alive. The perception was so strange but real. I began to weep from the depths of my soul.

I had never experienced this kind of fear or pain before. I tried to dismiss it as being too sentimental about our unique occurrence.

Before I conclude this chapter, I must highlight how the Lord prepared me for this moment for over two years. After I committed my life to Jesus, I embarked on a resolute journey to live by God's principles. My baptism in 1980 kindled an incredible thirst for understanding the God I had surrendered to. Many people make that same commitment to Christ but need to improve in their dedication. During their surrender, they sing the familiar old song, "Just as I Am," only to leave just as they came. They go home and sow their wild oats, six days a week, and then return to church on Sunday to pray for a crop failure. Their devotion remains superficial, a path I was determined not to tread.

Therefore, I immersed myself in daily Bible study. I began with the book of Proverbs and used an easy-to-read version known as the Living Bible. My appetite for spiritual wisdom knew no bounds. I delved into the works of renowned Christian authors such as Chuck Swindoll, Adrian Rogers, Max Lucado, John MacArthur, Charles Stanley, A.W. Tozer, Leonard Ravenhill, Joel Osteen, James Robinson, John Hagee, Joyce Meyer, Beth Moore, Warren Wiersbe, Jerry Bridges, Steve Farrar, and countless others.

Although I appreciated the pastors and teachers who taught me on Sundays, the Holy Spirit was my best teacher. He taught me how to interpret and apply the verses I meditated on daily. The Lord dealt one-on-one with me as He did with the Apostle Paul in 2 Corinthians 12:2-5. Therefore, my spiritual life grew stronger daily, and my heart became more tender to people.

By being consistent in God's word, I emerged like velvet and steel through daily renewal in His presence. The Holy Spirit metamorphosed me like a butterfly coming out of a cocoon. Love replaced my hatred, and my sadness was exchanged for joy. God's peace soothed my anxieties. My short fuse was transformed with patience, my anger with kindness, my fickle heart with faithfulness, my wild nature for a gentle soul, and my self-centeredness was exchanged for self-control.

However, lest one think that I am saying that I had it all together or that I had reached perfection, let me be clear: by no means! If my life were a pencil, it would be six inches of eraser and a quarter-inch lead. (More on that later.) It was phenomenal how the Holy Spirit sent despondent and disillusioned people to me for encouragement and guidance. I repeat: I did not arrange these meetings; they were led to me—divine appointments, if you will.

To my surprise, with God's help, I could encourage and counsel them, and I remembered Bible verses that gave them support and consolation and put the wind back into their sails. It is because I had been where they were and comforted them with the same comfort I had been given. Like it says in 2 Corinthians 1:3-4:

"All praise to God, the Father of our Lord Jesus Christ. God is our merciful Father and the source of all comfort. He comforts us in all our troubles so that we can comfort others. When they are troubled, we can give them the same comfort God has given us."

Giving help to others kept me on my toes and made me stronger. As fate would have it, this anchor of my soul proved to be the thing that would pull me through the significant life change I was about to experience.

It was Tuesday, March 15, 1982, and I was doing my morning devotional Bible meditation. I read a verse I had meditated on many times before, but it was different this time. It was as if a piece of black paper had been placed around it to block out all other verses; it was luminous. Out of nowhere, the verse was (Philippians 4:13 NKJV): "I can do all things through Christ who strengthens me."

As I continued to read, I landed on another Bible verse with the same luminous appearance. The words were from 2 Corinthians 12:8-9 NLT:

"I begged the Lord to take it away three times. Each time, he said, 'My grace is all you need. My power works best in weakness.' So now I am glad to boast about my weaknesses so that the power of Christ can work through me."

The sweet Lord used those two verses to combine forces in my heart and revealed that something tough was coming but that I would find strength and peace through it. He was saying, 'a trial was coming, but I've got you!'

Like a bolt of lightning, it hit me. Dad! I looked down at my roommate lying on the floor; he was in preparation for a test. Then I realized that I, too, had been in preparation for the biggest test of my life, but was unaware of it. I said, "Kent, my dad died."

"What? How do you know that? Why would you say that?" he retorted.

“I believe God has prepared me for this moment for the past two years. I cannot explain it; I just know.”

About five minutes later came the ominous ring of the phone. It was my brother. He spoke sombrely and said, “Mark, it’s your brother, Rick. Something has happened, and I am coming to pick you up.”

“It’s Dad, isn’t it?” I responded.

“We will talk when I arrive Mark.” Rick said in somber tone.

I told him, “Save yourself the trouble; I can drive home.” I just needed to gather my things. After we hung up, I went outside for some fresh air. While I prayed, I asked the Lord for a particular request:

Firstly, I thanked Him for preparing me for this moment and for our last words being filled with mutual love and respect. Then I said, “Heavenly Father, I recognize this as my greatest test, but I trust your guidance. I have one simple request—let me sense your strong, comforting embrace; for you have promised to be near to the broken-hearted” (Psalm 34:18).

By my usual routine, I would have been headed to the gym to work out at this time. I had a training partner that was 6’6” tall and built like a fire hydrant. He was so strong that you could feel your shoelaces tighten when he shook your hand. He was one of the strongest men I have ever met. But when it came to our workouts, he was always late. But not today!

To my surprise, my training partner arrived early for a change, unaware of my inner turmoil. I concluded my prayer, and he saw my pained expression and tearful eyes as he approached. He remained silent as his powerful arms enveloped me like a protective shield, as one would embrace a child. The realization of such a tangible hug was surreal, and it was as if Jesus had dispatched a consoling angel at the precise moment that I needed one. That day, God’s presence became so real to me because He answered my plea with impeccable timing.

Before recounting the subsequent incident, let me share something about my dad. When fear or pain gripped me in my childhood, he'd draw near and assure me, saying, "It's okay, son. Ole' dad is right here; everything will be just fine." Ironically, the Lord has used my dad's words, which have echoed in my life numerous times.

After I packed for the return home, a sense of sadness and emotion overwhelmed me. I took a seat on the bed and exhaled for relief. Then, all of a sudden, I sensed an immense, warm, sturdy hand on my shoulder. My first thought was that it was my training partner once more. Yet, as I reached for the hand to acknowledge his presence, I found no one there. To this day, I hold onto the belief that, in that moment, another comforting angel was sent to reassure me that His presence would forever be near. Once again, the familiar words resounded: "It's okay, son. Ole' dad is right here; everything will be just fine."

Think not thou canst sigh a sigh, and thy Maker is not by:
Think not thou canst weep a tear, and thy Maker is not near.
William Blake[9]

Finally, I want to close this chapter with one more amazing thing God did for me during this painful time. After the funeral, I went into a large dark closet and said another specific prayer. I prayed, "Lord, I believe I will make it through this dark valley, but only if you walk with me. Please, Father, take me by the hand and guide me one day at a time."

The moment after I made this request, I needed to gain some strength and reassurance. So, I opened my Bible and began to read. I landed on:

---

[9] Blake, W. (n.d.). *On Another's Sorrow*. Poem Analysis. Retrieved August 21, 2024, from https://poemanalysis.com/william-blake/on-anothers-sorrow/

(Isaiah 41:10 NASB):
"Do not fear, for I am with you; Do not anxiously look about you, for I am your God. I will strengthen you, and I will help you; I will uphold you with My righteous right hand."

This life-altering experience is just the start of God's demonstration of His presence in my life. Do you harbor painful sorrows? Have you endured the loss of a loved one? Have you weathered a painful breakup or struggled through a relentless illness? Have you wondered and worried about your child's X-ray? Have you faced the stark reality of job loss or experienced the sting of rejection from those you held closest to? Be assured He yearns to make His presence known to you. All it takes is your earnest search and a child's faith to pour your heart out to Him. He awaits your call for assistance. Today is the day!

"God is our refuge and strength, a very present help in trouble." —Isaiah 46:1 NLT

 [10]

Digital depiction of our last goodbye.

Takeaways and Lessons Learned:

It is easy to understand why part 2 of this book is titled *When God Becomes Real.* These are the lessons the author gained when his dad went to Heaven:

1. The Bible supernaturally prepared Mark for this loss and others to come. The Lord orchestrated a time when their last words were full of love, appreciation, and respect.
2. God answered Mark's prayer and met his need for strong, compassionate arms and a soothing embrace by sending his large, muscular friend at just the right moment. Mark believes that it was an Angel that touched his shoulder and whispered his dad's words to his broken heart.
3. The Lord also answered Mark's prayer "to hold his hand and guide him" in Isaiah 41.

[10] Tool, D. E. (2024). Saying Goodbye to Dad [Digital image]. Online. OpenAI. (2024). ChatGPT (4o) [Large language model]. https://chatgpt.com/c/67956650-b0da-4db0-a561-08825e073d46

Reflection Questions for Application:

1. **How Have I Experienced God's Presence in My Darkest Moments?**
   - Reflect on times in your life when you faced significant loss or hardship. How did you feel God's presence and comfort during those times? Consider specific moments when you sensed divine intervention or reassurance.
2. **How Can I Strengthen My Relationship with God During Times of Peace?**
   - Think about your spiritual practices and how they prepare you for future challenges. How can you deepen your relationship with God during calm times to build a foundation of faith that will sustain you during difficult periods?
3. **How Can I Offer Comfort to Others in Their Time of Need?**
   - Reflect on ways you can support others experiencing loss or hardship. How can you use your own experiences of God's comfort to provide empathy, understanding, and encouragement to struggling people? Consider practical steps you can take to be a source of light and hope in someone else's dark days.

5

Divine Replacement

How God Filled My Fatherless Void

Reflecting on my life's extraordinary journey, I'm humbled by the supernatural orchestrations that unfolded after my father's passing. Amidst the grief and the stressful pursuit of higher education, fate had a divinely planned encounter that would eternally shape my destiny.

In this chapter, I have the privilege to share the amazing story of how the Lord replaced the absence of my earthly father with a man who would become my spiritual father—Bill Bryan, who was even the same age as my father.

It was the summer of 1982, just a few months after my dad crossed to his eternal home. I was a personal trainer at the renowned International Fitness Club, next door to the Appleseed Health Store. One day, a seemingly mundane trip to the neighboring vitamin and supplement shop would change my destiny forever.

Unaware of the divine appointment awaiting me, I entered Bill's establishment. Our eyes met, and an immediate connection sparked between us. It was as if our souls recognized each other, transcending the years that separated us in age. We became kindred spirits bonded by our shared faith and genuine love for God.

Our similarities were uncanny—from facial expressions to humor and our mutual passion for bodybuilding. A week earlier, I had won a seven-state contest and dedicated the trophy to my ailing father, who always encouraged me to "go show them what a country boy made of meat and potatoes can do."

Bill and I exchanged stories and training routines, losing track of time as three hours flew by. It felt like I was interacting with an older and wiser version of myself.

Little did I know that Pastor Bryan would become my spiritual father, guiding me and shaping God's incredible future in store for me. In his presence, I found solace and acceptance. It was evident that the Heavenly Father had handpicked him to fill the void left by my earthly father's absence.

Laughter became the hallmark of our relationship. The time we spent together was always filled with booming uproar, joy, and funny stories that infected everyone around us. It was as if God delighted in our friendship. We brought out the best in each other, finding strength and rejuvenation in shared moments of light-heartedness. Through laughter, life's burdens were lifted, and our spirits soared.

Brother Bill often mentioned that God had put us together for a twofold blessing: for him and me. He had lost some of his "mojo," and the Holy Spirit used me to help reignite his passion.

Yet, he was more than a joyful companion; he was also a powerful preacher—a vessel through which God's Word flowed with authority and anointing. His unique gift for teaching the Bible without relying on notes made it feel like the voice of God spoke straight to the spirit of each listener, transforming and comforting thousands of lives through his teachings.

Bill emphasized that he preferred to call his talks "messages" rather than sermons, believing that a message born in the heart would reach the heart, but a sermon born in the head only reaches the head. He wanted to give people more than three points and a poem of homiletical discourse.

What set him apart was his lack of formal seminary education. He often joked, "I've never been to cemetery," emphasizing that some focused so much on higher learning and degrees that they lost the true meaning of ministry as Jesus intended. He would say, "There are so many doctors in the pulpits, you would think God was sick." Bill's humor, life stories, and authenticity made him a beloved speaker in hundreds of churches.

Our relationship mirrored the deep connections between biblical mentors like 'Elijah and Elisha', and 'Paul and Timothy'. Under his mentorship, my spiritual journey deepened. His guidance refined my character, strengthened my faith, and deepened my understanding of God's Word.

With his encouragement, I became more purposeful, discovering the voice God had placed within me. Recognizing this calling, Bill took me under his wing, nurturing and equipping me to let the Holy Spirit speak through me. Sometimes, he'd surprise me on Sunday mornings, saying, "You're preaching today." At first, I'd feel anxious. I would give a popcorn testimony, pop up, and turn white. But over time, I began to share what The Lord was teaching me with confidence and be led by the Holy Spirit.

What had once been my greatest fear now brought me the most joy—standing in front of a crowd without notes, offering comfort, encouragement, and faith, leading them to Jesus, and sharing laughter.

Bill Bryan's impact on my life was immeasurable, and the lessons I learned from him extended beyond preaching and teaching. Bill believed that being a pastor was just the cherry on top; authentic ministry was in serving people. He often quoted Mark 9:35, emphasizing the need to be a servant to all.

We had a respectable reputation in our little mountain town. People saw us as father and son, working tirelessly in hay fields, helping local farmers and ranchers without expecting anything in return. We branded cattle, built fences, fixed machinery, and helped with irrigation. We'd come home exhausted, but fulfilled, developing deep friendships within the community.

He encouraged me to tend to the needs of older widows, teaching me the significance of compassion and authentic servanthood. He introduced me to nursing homes and prison ministries, where we offered comfort and shared tears and laughter with those in need.

Our good reputation in our little village drew many to our old-fashioned country church. It resembled a Norman Rockwell painting, with wooden pews, a potbelly stove, coal oil lights, and a pine mourners' bench. Over time, we updated it while preserving its charm.

I eventually became the youth leader, growing the ministry from a simple hayride and bonfire to seventy consistent attendees on Saturday nights. I shared with these teens the lessons on servanthood I'd learned from him.

Just as Paul considered Timothy ready to travel and minister alone, Brother Bill felt the same about me. I received a call out of nowhere. A nearby Wesleyan Church in need of an interim pastor received my name as a possible choice. I agreed to serve, emphasizing my commitment to teaching the Bible rather than church doctrine.

Bill and I knelt in prayer, knowing an era was ending. At twenty-two years old, I served as their pastor after their confirmation and ordination.

The following chapters reveal how God continued to lead me to higher ground. Although I missed my spiritual father, we stayed connected, bringing our churches together for all-night sing-a-longs and prayer. Bill Bryan, who lived to be ninety-four, departed in 2021. He left this world with his heart at peace. His impact on my life remains immeasurable, and I am forever grateful. **(Philippians 2:22 NIV)** - "But you know that Timothy has proved himself because as a son with his father, he has served with me in the work of the gospel."

Brother Bill Bryan- My Spiritual father [11]

3' x 5' OIL Painting by Mark Bruton

[11] Bruton, M. W. Tool, D. E. (2024). Brother Bill Reading the Word [Photograph]. Online. OpenAI. (2024). ChatGPT (4o) [Large language model]. https://chatgpt.com/c/1cb7f7ec-6b42-4603-a436-2f25698f6653

The old country church where it all began - 1982

Takeaways and Lessons Learned:

1. **Embrace the Word:** Like Bill Bryan, let us approach the Bible with diligence and devotion, daily seeking to understand it, line upon line, verse upon verse. Let us allow the Bible to be our daily guide and foundation by making it the first part of every day and trusting the Holy Spirit to lead us in everything we do. (**See Proverbs 3:5-6**).
2. **Impact through Service:** Bill's example shows the power of serving others beyond the pulpit. Let us follow suit by finding ways to serve and care for those in our church and

community, especially the vulnerable and elderly, reflecting Christ's love in practical ways.

3. **Mentorship Matters:** Bill's role as a spiritual father highlights the importance of mentorship in the Christian journey. Let us seek and embrace mentorship relationships and be willing to mentor and disciple others, passing on wisdom, love, service, and spiritual insights.

Reflection and Application Questions:

1. How can you cultivate a deeper understanding of the Bible and allow the Holy Spirit to guide your life and ministry, just as Bill Bryan did?
2. How can you serve and care for the unique needs of your church, families, and communities beyond the confines of traditional religion?
3. Reflecting on Bill's mentorship, how can you become spiritual fathers and mothers to others, investing in their spiritual growth and journey?

6

The University of Adversity

Becoming Stronger through Growing Pains

Between 1982 and 1993, the Lord enrolled me into the University of Adversity. This school differed from the path I would have chosen, and the lessons were often difficult. The tuition for this school was high. Yet, it was a scholarship from the Heavenly Father, offering a unique opportunity for growth.

In this chapter, I will share a condensed version of my challenges and the profound lessons I learned. While a complete account would take years to narrate, I will share the transformative highlights of my journey.

Professor Holy Spirit offered invaluable and life-altering courses at this spiritual institution, each designed to bring growth. Here are a few:

Course Syllabus:

101: From Pain to Purpose: Unveiling the Hidden Blessings of Adversity.
102: Struggles of the Heart: Finding Hope and Strength in Calamity.
103: Facing the Storms: Navigating Turbulent Waters.
104: Fires of Refinement: How Trials Molded My Character.
105: Building on The Rock: The Foundation of Faith During Hardship.

106: Losses and Gains: Discovering Strength through Setbacks.
107: From Darkness to Light: Hold on to Jesus in Times of Despair.

Many people graduate from this school ***Suma Cum Laude.*** I graduated; ***"Thank the Laude!"*** We all remain alumni of this university, and sometimes, we must take a few upper-level refresher courses. Here are some of my continuing development classes:

Post-graduate Courses:

304: Restoring the Wayward: Growing through God's Chastening Hand.
402: Back to the Woodshed: Accept God's Loving Correction.
407: Lessons in Humility: How Heartaches Shape Us into Christ's Image.

"Just one more rep, Steve," we shout to our training partner. Why? When our strength fails, and we are willing to push through the pain, we achieve maximum gains and become bigger, faster, and stronger. Over time, it becomes evident that we've made tremendous progress.

People observe our determination to welcome the discomfort and exhaustion required for this progress. Thus, anyone aspiring to be physically strong and fit must embrace this demanding ordeal and surpass their limits to attain their goal.

The same principle applies in the spiritual realm: "No pain, no gain!" Learning to push through the difficulty is why the Lord permits all individuals to undergo trials and heartaches. However, the extent may vary, depending on God's purpose for each person.

For instance, those who serve as the most effective comforters for someone battling cancer are often individuals who have faced or are facing cancer themselves. Likewise, those who have undergone similar trauma form the most empathetic connections with children who have experienced abuse.

In 2 Corinthians 1:4, the Bible reminds us that God comforts us in our tribulations so that we can do the same for others.

Someone has said, "Trials can either make us bitter or better." You see, friend, the problems life throws our way aren't the issue; how we respond to them matters.

It's all about personal choice. Many people opt for bitterness, constantly questioning the Heavenly Father, "Why, God? Why me?" But the strongest and most resilient individuals are the ones who declare, "Father, I will trust you even though I don't understand." This attitude is not innate; it's cultivated in adversity. The forthcoming events describe some of my trials and lessons learned at the University of Adversity.

The Last Ride

Firstly, let me tell you about my younger brother, Jimmy, who may have been small and slender, but his fearlessness and tenacity were second to none. He was so thin that you could've used him for dental floss! I'd tease him, saying, "Jimmy, you have to tickle the hair on your legs just to keep from sliding into your socks."

But he was a true cowboy, through and through. Despite his size, he was tougher than the back wall of a shooting gallery, and he could tie most men into a Japanese Ground Knot in no time. He had a knack for making us all laugh when he jammed his big five-gallon hat onto his little one-gallon head, causing his ears to stick out and fold down.

At twenty-one years old, he was a rising star and very popular on the rodeo circuit, a bull rider of great skill. But tragedy struck in the cruel year of 1984.

I remember the night all too well. The sun dipped below the horizon as Jimmy's name was announced. The crowd cheered, and the air filled with the scent of popcorn, hay, manure, and dust. Beer bottles clattered together as the gate swung open, and the bull exploded into the arena.

Little Jim clung to its back, the crowd's cheers turning to gasps as the bull bucked violently, flinging him into the sky. He hit the ground with a sickening thud, and a horrified silence fell over the stands.

The bull's hooves pounded Jim into the earth, each impact reverberating through the bleachers. Women screamed, and dust filled the arena as medics rushed to Jimmy's side.

The festive atmosphere vanished, replaced by dread. Seeing my brother still on the ground and hauled away in an ambulance was heartbreaking for those who knew Jimmy. Many in the crowd dispersed slowly; the weight of the tragedy was heavy in the air. Just like that, he was gone.

Faced with questioning God or trusting Him, I chose the latter. In my grief, I prayed and asked how anything good could come from this. But then, I witnessed a miracle: countless rugged cowboys heard the Gospel at Jimmy's funeral, leading several to accept Christ. From this tragedy, God turned something terrible into something life-changing, reinforcing my faith and trust in Him.

These losses continued as my family and I bid farewell to my father, grandfathers, grandmothers, my sister Vandi, my brother Rick, and numerous aunts and uncles. With each loss, my heart grew stronger, my empathy deeper, and my compassion more Christ-like. The pain of these events yielded significant gains, fortifying me to face future trials.

"I walked a mile with pleasure, and she chatted all the way
But left me none the wiser for all she had to say.
I walked a mile with sorrow, and ne'er a word said she.
But, oh! The things I learned from her when
sorrow walked with me."

— Robert Browning Hamilton [12]

Sister's Faith: Living Fully Even in Adversity

The journey of my sister, Vandi, had the most life-changing impact on me. She was diagnosed with a devastating Glioblastoma brain tumor at the age of twenty-eight; she faced this battle with unconquerable faith.

Despite the grim prognosis of only six months to live, Vandi refused to accept a death sentence. Her love for her three daughters, including one with Down syndrome, fueled her fierce fight and defiance of the odds.

After her first brain surgery, the hospital room hummed with machines and a scent that was a mix of antiseptics and the faint aroma of lavender from Vandi's potpourri pot.

Sunlight streamed through the window, casting a warm glow over her frail form. Despite the paleness of her skin, the large head bandage, and the evident toll of the treatments, Vandi's eyes sparkled with an unyielding spirit.

Whenever her three daughters visited, their laughter and playful energy filled the room and were her lifeline. Even the oldest, with Down syndrome, seemed to understand the gravity of the situation, offering endless hugs and kisses. The soft rustling of coloring books

---

[12] Hamilton, R. B. (2023). I walked a mile with Pleasure (1st ed.). Good Reads-Online. https://www.goodreads.com/quotes/289683-i-walked-a-mile-with-pleasure-she-chatted-all-the

and the occasional giggles provided a backdrop to Vandi's happy place in this violent storm of her life.

One morning, I watched Sis gently pull clumps of her long, beautiful hair, the strands falling silently onto her lap. With tears in her eyes, she looked upward and smiled. "Even so, Lord, I still praise You," she whispered, her voice as steady as her resolve. The room seemed to hold its breath, the air thick with the scent of lavender and the sound of faith.

"Sis, we are in awe of your strength and trust in God amidst all of this," I said, my voice barely a whisper. She responded by softly quoting the words of the song, **God on The Mountain**, by Traci Dartt.

"Life is easy when you're up on the mountain,
And you've got peace of mind like you've never known.
But things change when you're down in the valley,
Don't lose faith, for you're never alone.
For the God on the mountain is still God in the valley,
When things go wrong, He'll make them right.
And the God of the good times is still God in the bad times;
The God of the day is still God in the night.
You talk of faith when you're up on the mountain,
But talk comes so easy when life is at its best.
It's down in the valleys of trials and temptations,
That's where your faith is really put to the test.
For the God on the mountain is still God in the valley.
When things go wrong, He'll make them right,
And the God of the good times is still God in the bad times.
The God of the day is still God in the night."[13]

---

[13] Randle, L., & Dartt, T. (n.d.). *God On the Mountain*. Genius. Retrieved August 21, 2024, from https://genius.com/Lynda-randle-god-on-the-mountain-lyrics/q/writer

Her voice, though weakened, filled the room with a serene strength, wrapping us in a cocoon of calm amidst the storm of her illness.

Doctors and nurses often marveled at her. "There's something very different about Vandi," they would say. Sis refused to sit, sulk, and sour. Instead, she spent her days comforting fellow patients, her touch bringing an unexpected warmth. She would crawl into their beds to read an excerpt from a Chuck Swindoll book, **"The Hammer, The File, and the Furnace."** Her voice was always a soothing balm in the clinical, sterile environment.

Once released from the hospital, Sis didn't retreat. Instead, she returned often to bring hope and compassion to the sick and hurting, her visits marked by the smell of freshly baked goods and the sound of heartfelt laughter. Her life became a testament to the power of selflessness, teaching me that focusing on others' pain could lighten our own burdens.

Vandi defied the odds by God's grace and lived five more years. Each day was a treasure, filled with the scent of flowers, the taste of home-cooked meals, and the sound of her three daughters' laughter.

Sis often said, "There is an eternal destiny in the present moment." Her words became a guiding light in my own life and ministry.

Her final day in 1987 was a blend of quiet and profound peace. She had been comatose for three months with no expression, her once vibrant presence now still. We all realized that she was holding on for the sake of her girls. So, while holding her hand, I whispered, "It's okay, Sis. It's time to go home now; Jesus is waiting for you with open arms." The girls will be ok.

Tears streamed down her cheeks, and a serene smile spread across her face as she pointed as if she was seeing something beautiful beyond our world. Her final breath was a release, a peaceful transition that left an indelible mark on all of us.

Vandi's daughters have grown into remarkable women, and their success is a living testament to her enduring influence. Her legacy of faith and love inspires us to live fully and express our love without hesitation.

Reflecting on her journey, I'm reminded of Reba McEntire's song, **"Last Walk in the Rain,"**[14] which strongly reminds us of life's fleeting nature and the importance of living in the moment. I encourage you to take a few minutes to listen to it.

My time at the University of Adversity taught me invaluable lessons about faith and empathy. My sister's remarkable faith and selflessness were beacons, showing that adversity can make us better, not bitter.

As we navigate life's challenges, let us embrace each moment, knowing that there is an eternal destiny in every heartbeat. Our time on this earth is short; let us make the most of it by embracing each day as a gift from God.

"Rain, rain, beating hard against the pane,
How endlessly it pours out of doors.
From the darkening sky, I question why,
But then, flowers, flowers, blooming fresh and fair, everywhere!
Ah, now God has explained why it rained."

—Author unknown. [15]

---

[14] McEntire, R. (2008, February 1). *If I had only known.* LYRICS. Retrieved August 8, 2023, from https://www.lyrics.com/lyric/30201544/Reba+McEntire/If+I+Had+Only+Known#google_vignette

[15] Cowman, L. (2008). Poem, Rain, Rain (3rd ed.). Zondervan. (2008). Streams in The Desert (3rd ed.). Zondervan. https://www.amazon.com/s?i=stripbooks&rh=p_27%3AL.+B.+E.+Cowman&s=relevancerank&text=L.+B.+E.+Cowman&ref=dp_byline_sr_book_1

[16]

Digital Depictions

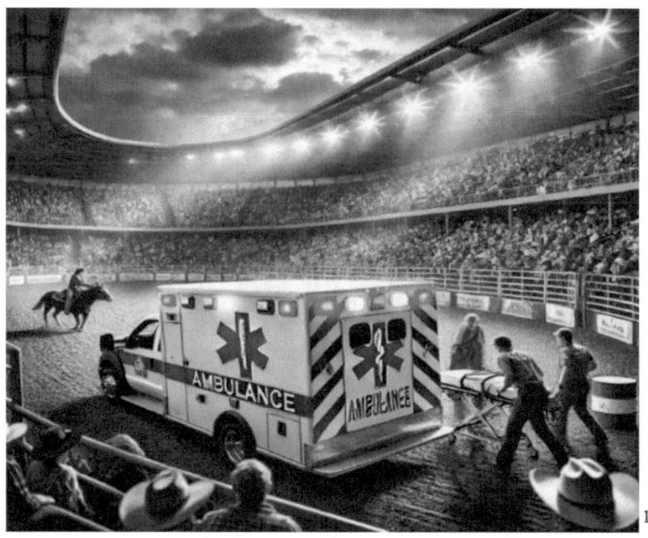

[17]

[16] Tool, D. E. (2024). University Of Adversity [Digital image]. ONLINE. OpenAI. (2024). ChatGPT (4o) [Large language model]. https://chatgpt.com/c/30da19ab-5766-489c-8989-31f7f5ae831b

[17] Tool, D. E. (2024). My Brothers Rodeo Accident- "Last Ride" [Digital image]. ONLINE. OpenAI. (2024). ChatGPT (4o) [Large language model]. https://chatgpt.com/c/b7dd579d-77b0-4696-91c7-0eb9978233e3

Digital Depiction of my brother's accident

[18]

Digital Depictions of Vandi

[19]

Going Home

[18] Tool, D. E. (2024). Depiction of Vandi [Photograph]. Online. OpenAI. (2024). ChatGPT (4o) [Large language model]. https://chatgpt.com/c/67956650-b0da-4db0-a561-08825e073d46'

[19] Tool, D. E. (2024). Vandi Goes Home To Heaven [Digital image]. Online. OpenAI. (2024). ChatGPT (4o) [Large language model]. https://chatgpt.com/c/67956650-b0da-4db0-a561-08825e073d46

Takeaways and Lessons Learned:

1. **Embrace Adversity as a Tool for Growth:** The chapter emphasizes that life's challenges and hardships are not meant to break us but to shape and strengthen us. The author's journey through the University of Adversity showcases how difficult times can lead to profound personal and spiritual growth, transforming pain into purpose.
2. **Faith and Trust in God during Hardships:** Through the author's experiences, we learn that maintaining faith and trust in God, even when we do not understand the reasons behind our suffering, is crucial. Trusting God's plan and believing He can bring good out of any situation is a recurring lesson throughout the chapter.
3. **The Power of Selflessness and Compassion:** The author's sister, Vandi, is a powerful example of living a life of faith and selflessness despite personal suffering. Her focus on comforting others even while battling a terminal illness teaches us the importance of looking beyond our pain to help others, which can bring healing to our hearts.

Reflection Questions for Application:

1. **How Can I Find Purpose in My Adversities?**
   - Reflect on the challenges you are currently facing or have faced in the past. How can you reframe these difficulties to see them as opportunities for growth and learning? Consider specific ways to turn your pain into a source of strength and purpose.
2. **In What Ways Can I Deepen My Trust in God During Tough Times?**
   - Think about how you respond to adversity. Do you question God, or do you trust He has a plan for you?

Reflect on ways to strengthen your faith and trust in God's goodness, even when circumstances are complicated or unclear.

3. **How Can I Show Compassion to Others amid My Struggles?**
   - Consider how you can use your experiences of pain and hardship to empathize with and support others going through similar challenges. What practical steps can you take to reach out and offer comfort and encouragement to those in need, just as Vandi did? Reflect on how focusing on others can bring healing to your own heart.

7

God's Prescription Pad

Bible Verses that Teach Us How to Be Godfident

[20]

(Doctor Jesus, 2024)

For years, I have longed to share the stories in this book. My goal is to leave a legacy of faith that will inspire my children, grandchildren, and anyone who needs a boost in fully trusting our Heavenly Father.

These chapters contain my personal narratives, each a testament to God's miraculous power in my life. Join me on this life adventure,

[20] Tool, D. E. (2024). Doctor Jesus [Digital image]. Online. OpenAI. (2024). ChatGPT (4o) [Large language model]. https://chatgpt.com/c/f6aafc73-2866-4a1c-b125-8d524968f22e?model=gpt-4o

and you will witness my transformation from self-reliance to unwavering 'Godfidence'——a profound trust in His ability to change circumstances in an instant.

Through the pages ahead, you'll encounter my 'Bragimony,' where boasting about my achievements gives way to celebrating God's unmatched ability to reshape our lives. This transition is a beacon of hope, showing that there's always room for growth and change no matter where you are in your faith, whether you are a new convert or an old, seasoned Bible scholar.

Someone said, "You can depend on God for your future, based upon His performance in your past." This saying has become my life's anthem.

In the following encounters, you'll see prayers answered in unimaginable ways, doors opened by God's hand, and divine alignments beyond comprehension.

Delve into these stories, and may you be inspired to relinquish control and depend wholly on the One who holds your destiny. Remember, just as the Heavenly Father has guided me, He is also ready to guide you in your life voyage.

Isaiah 30:18 - NIV: "*The Lord longs to be gracious to you.*"

Have you ever stood at a crossroads, uncertain of the right path, doubting your ability to face the challenges before you? Follow me into the chapters ahead. In these moments—where wondrous answers to prayer unfolded, supernatural appointments occurred, and doors swung open—is where my "Godfidence" was born.

Friend, you are about to walk paths where serendipity meets sovereignty. Here, God's astonishing life arrangements appear in unexpected and awe-inspiring ways, leaving no room for boasting except in the Lord.

Get ready to be surprised by the unexpected ways the Holy Spirit can work in your life. May your soul be ignited with the revelation that the same God who guided my past longs to lead you into all of your tomorrows, brimming with His boundless goodness and grace.

The next chapter will explore these amazing, jaw-dropping encounters. But before beginning, allow me to take the symbolic role of a physician with a prescription pad.

Just as we need a doctor's diagnosis to prescribe the right medicine, we also need the Great physician's guidance for our spiritual well-being. Consider the following verses as God's prescription for cultivating "Godfidence" in our lives.

Godfidence is the medicine, and these scriptures are the recommendations from Dr. Jesus. Please meditate on each passage and **insert your name into the verses**, as this will prepare you for the exciting journey that awaits:

Malachi 3:10 - NIV

"Test me in this, says the Lord Almighty, and see if I will not throw open the floodgates of heaven and pour out so much blessing that there will not be room enough to store it."

Jeremiah 29:11-13 NLT

"For I know the plans I have for you," says the Lord. "They are plans for good and not for disaster, to give you a future and a hope. In those days when you pray, I will listen. If you look for me wholeheartedly, you will find me. "

Zechariah 4: 6-7 - NLT

"Then he said to me, "This is what the Lord says to Zerubbabel: It is not by force nor by strength, but by my Spirit, says the Lord of Heaven's Armies. Nothing, not even a mighty mountain, will stand in Zerubbabel's way…."

Isaiah 43: 1-4 - NLT

But now, O Jacob, listen to the Lord who created you. O Israel, the one who formed you, says, "Do not be afraid, for I have ransomed you. I have called you by name; you are mine. When you go through deep waters, I will be with you. When you go through rivers of difficulty, you will not drown. When you walk through the fire of oppression, you will not be burned up; the flames will not consume you. For I am the Lord, your God, the Holy One of Israel, your Savior… "Do not be afraid, for I am with you.

Joshua 1: 7-9 - NLT

"Be strong and very courageous. Be careful to obey all the instructions Moses gave you. Do not deviate from them, turning either to the right or to the left. Then, you will be successful in everything you do. Study this Book of Instruction continually. Meditate on it day and night so you will be sure to obey everything written in it. Only then will you prosper and succeed in all you do. 9 This is my command—be strong and courageous! Do not be afraid or discouraged. For the Lord your God is with you wherever you go."

In the next verse, you will read the account of when the twelve spies scouted and explored the land of Canaan. Notice that only Joshua and Caleb had Godfidence.

Numbers 13: 27-33 – NLT

This was their report to Moses: "We entered the land you sent us to explore, and it is indeed a bountiful country—a land flowing with milk and honey. Here is the kind of fruit it produces. 28 But the people living there are powerful, and their towns are large and fortified. We even saw giants there, the descendants of Anak! 29 The Amalekites live in the Negev, and the Hittites, Jebusites, and Amorites live in the hill country. The Canaanites live along the coast of the Mediterranean Sea and along the Jordan Valley."

30 **But Caleb** tried to quiet the people as they stood before Moses. **"Let's go at once to take the land," he said. "We can certainly conquer it!" -** ***(GODFIDENCE)***

31 But the other men who had explored the land with him
disagreed. "We can't go up against them! They are stronger than we
are!" 32 So they spread this bad report about the land among the
Israelites: "The land we traveled through and explored will devour
anyone who goes to live there. All the people we saw were huge. 33
We even saw giants there, the descendants of Anak. Next to them, we
felt like grasshoppers, and that's what they thought, too!" (Emphasis
mine)

Psalm 112: 7-9 - NLT

"…Those who are righteous will be long remembered. 7 They do
not fear bad news; they confidently trust the Lord to care for them. 8
They are confident and fearless and can face their foes triumphantly.
9 They share freely and give generously to those in need. Their good
deeds will be remembered forever. They will have influence and
honor." (Emphasis mine)

Psalm 16: 7-9 – NLT

7 "I will bless the Lord who guides me; even at night my heart
instructs me. 8 I know the Lord is always with me. I will not be
shaken, for He is right beside me. 9 No wonder my heart is glad, and
I rejoice. My body rests in safety."

Psalm 27:1-3 - NLT

"The Lord is my light and my salvation— so why should I be
afraid? The Lord is my fortress, protecting me from danger, so why
should I tremble? 2 When evil people come to devour me, when my
enemies and foes attack me, they will stumble and fall. 3 Though a
mighty army surrounds me, my heart will not be afraid. Even if I am
attacked, I will remain confident."

Psalm 33: 20-22 – NLT: “We put our hope in the Lord. He is our help and our shield. 21 In him our hearts rejoice, for we trust in his holy name. 22 Let your unfailing love surround us, Lord, for our hope is in you alone.”

Psalm 34:1-10 – NLT: 1 I will praise the Lord at all times. I will constantly speak his praises. 2 I will boast only in the Lord; let all who are helpless take heart. 3 Come, let us tell of the Lord’s greatness; let us exalt his name together. 4 I prayed to the Lord, and he answered me. He freed me from all my fears. 5 Those who look to him for help will be radiant with joy; no shadow of shame will darken their faces. 6 In my desperation, I prayed, and the Lord listened; he saved me from all my troubles. 7 For the angel of the Lord is a guard; he surrounds and defends all who fear him. 8 Taste and see that the Lord is good. Oh, the joys of those who take refuge in him! 9 Fear the Lord, you, his godly people, for those who fear him will have all they need. 10 Even strong young lions sometimes go hungry, but those who trust in the Lord will lack no good thing.

Psalm 34:17-19 – NLT:

17 “The Lord hears his people when they call to him for help. He rescues them from all their troubles. 18 The Lord is close to the brokenhearted; he rescues those whose spirits are crushed. 19 The righteous person faces many troubles, but the Lord comes to the rescue each time.”

Psalm 91: 1-4 – NLT:

1 Those who live in the shelter of the Most High will find rest in the shadow of the Almighty. 2 This I declare about the Lord: He alone is my refuge, my place of safety; He is my God, and I trust him. 3 He will rescue you from every trap and protect you from deadly disease. 4. He will cover you with his feathers. He will shelter you with his wings. His faithful promises are your armor and protection.

Psalm 91:14-16 – NLT:

14 The Lord says, "I will rescue those who love me. I will protect those who trust in my name. 15. I will answer when they call on me; I will be with them in trouble. I will rescue and honor them. 16 I will reward them with a long life and give them my salvation."

Psalm 118: 5-9 – NLT:

5 "In my distress, I prayed to the Lord, and the Lord answered me and set me free. 6 The Lord is for me, so I will have no fear. What can mere people do to me? 7 Yes, the Lord is for me; he will help me. I will look in triumph at those who hate me. 8 It is better to take refuge in the Lord than to trust in people. 9 It is better to take refuge in the Lord than to trust in princes."

Proverbs 3:5-6 – NLT:

5 Trust in the Lord with **all** your heart; do **not depend on your own understanding.** 6 Seek his will in **all** you do, and **he will show you which path to take.** (Emphasis mine)

Mathew 7: 7-10 – NLT: Jesus said-

7 "Keep on asking, and you will receive what you ask for. Keep on seeking, and you will find. Keep on knocking, and the door will be opened to you. **8** For everyone who asks receives. Everyone who seeks finds. And to everyone who knocks, the door will be opened. **9** "You parents—if your children ask for a loaf of bread, do you give them a stone instead? **10** Or if they ask for a fish, do you give them a snake? Of course not! **11** So if you sinful people know how to give good gifts to your children, how much more will your heavenly Father give good gifts to those who ask him."

Mark 11:22-25 – NLT:

22 Then Jesus said to the disciples, "Have faith in God. **23** I tell you the truth, you can say to this mountain, 'May you be lifted up

and thrown into the sea,' and it will happen. But you must really believe it will happen and have no doubt in your heart. **24** I tell you; you can pray for anything; if you believe you've received it, it will be yours. **25** But when you are praying, first forgive anyone you hold a grudge against, so that your Father in heaven will forgive your sins, too."

Philippians 4:6-7 – NLT:

6 "Don't worry about anything; instead, pray about everything. Tell God what you need specifically and thank him for all he has done. 7 Then you will experience God's peace, which exceeds anything we can understand. His peace will guard your hearts and minds as you live in Christ Jesus."

There you have it! The prescriptions for faith from the divine healer. Now, let us see how the medicine of faith works in real life.

Takeaways and Lessons Learned:

1. **Godfidence through Scripture**: The chapter emphasizes the importance of anchoring one's faith in the promises found in Scripture. By meditating on these verses, the author demonstrates how one can build "Godfidence"—a profound trust in God's ability to guide and transform our lives. This trust is not based on self-reliance but on the assurance that God is actively working in and through us.
2. **Personal Transformation and Testimony**: The author shares stories of how God has answered prayers and opened doors in unimaginable ways. These testimonies are powerful reminders that God is faithful and capable of performing miracles. The transformation from self-reliance to Godfidence is a journey marked by experiencing and recognizing God's hand in our everyday lives.

3. **Relinquishing Control to God**: The chapter encourages readers to relinquish their need for control and depend wholly on God. The author highlights that true faith involves trusting God's timing and plans, even when we don't understand them. This surrender allows God to work in our lives in ways we could never achieve ourselves.

Reflection Questions for Application:

1. **How Can I Build My Godfidence through Scripture?**
   - Reflect on the Bible verses provided in the chapter. How can you incorporate these scriptures into your daily life to build a deeper trust in God? Consider setting aside time daily to meditate on these verses and see how they strengthen your faith and confidence in God's plans.
2. **In What Areas of My Life Do I Need to Relinquish Control to God?**
   - Think about aspects of your life where you may be holding on too tightly and relying on your own strength. How can you practice surrendering these areas to God and trusting Him to lead you? Reflect on specific steps you can take to let go and let God work in your life.
3. **How Has God Demonstrated His Faithfulness in My Past?**
   - Reflect on past experiences in which you have seen God's hand at work in your life. How can these experiences reinforce your trust in Him for your future? Consider journaling these testimonies as reminders of God's faithfulness and as a source of encouragement during challenging times.

8

Divine Encounters

Answered Prayers and Unexpected Blessings

The Widow and the Upper Room Apartment

As the semester ended in 1983, I yearned to return to my hometown and work through the summer. Finding a place to live was crucial. A church member mentioned an elderly widow renting an upper-room flat, which intrigued me. The Bible's words in **James 1:27- NLT** also came to mind:

"Pure and genuine religion in the sight of God the Father means caring for orphans and widows..."

Driven by this scripture, I arranged to meet the owner and inspect the lofted room.

A sunny Saturday morning greeted me; the air felt clean and crisp, and the birds sang cheerful melodies. The view from the street evoked nostalgia, and the old Victorian home appeared to belong in a storybook.

The dear older woman opened the door with a warm smile, her white hair gleaming in the sunlight.

"Please, come in," she beckoned, her voice soft and kind.

Upon entering, the scent of an older home and fresh-cut lilacs filled the room. The house also smelled of baked spice bread and freshly brewed coffee.

"Will you join me for coffee?" she invited.

"Yes, Ma'am, thank you kindly," I replied.

The woman, a family friend, and I knew each other from church, but we had never gotten acquainted. Her wisdom and her love for the Bible captivated me. We chatted for about half an hour, and then she offered to show me the attic living quarters.

"The room is up those stairs," she said, her eyes twinkling with kindness.

The steep staircase caught my attention. During the climb upward, I noticed that each step was polished and inviting, and my anticipation grew. The upper room dwelling featured angled ceilings creating cozy nooks, a charming living room bathed in soft morning light, and a cute little kitchen exuding warmth. But the nostalgic clawfoot bathtub captured my attention the most. The tub held significance because I had always wanted an old-fashioned clawfoot bathtub.

"How much is the rent, ma'am?" I inquired; my excitement tempered by the reality of my tight budget.

"It's $175 a month," she answered, "but you could do some handyman work in exchange for a lower rent."

Although it was an excellent offer, I didn't consider paying less. I agreed to help with the house repairs and pay the total amount, making it a win-win.

We completed the contract and shook hands to seal the deal. Each week, we shared a cup of tea as the aroma of chamomile and cinnamon rolls filled the air. We delved into deep conversations about the Bible. Her wisdom and close relationship with her Heavenly Father enveloped me like a warm blanket, making it one of the coziest homes I'd ever seen.

The summer ended, and the thought of leaving this dear woman and my beloved abode gnawed at me as I thought to myself, "Where will I find such a unique place for rent that low?"

My hopes dwindled with each fruitless newspaper ad I scanned. One afternoon, I poured out my distress to my friend Bonnie as she listened intently, her eyes full of understanding. She embodies a seasoned prayer warrior—a woman of devotion known for her prayer experience that yields results.

"Mark, I want to teach you something the Lord taught me long ago," she said. "Why don't you pray for the specific details of what you want and need? Remember, **Philippians 3:6-7** instructs us to be detailed and precise in our requests to our father above."

"Isn't that a little presumptuous?" I questioned, uncertainty in my voice.

She smiled. "Mark, think of it this way: A child asks for a bicycle, wouldn't the parents want to know the details of what they want? The color, the size, the brand?"

Inspired by her words, I began to pray. My voice shook at first, but my trust grew stronger as I offered up my supplications.

"Father, I thank you for already knowing my needs. Today, we come before you in Jesus' name to ask you for another upper-room living space for $175 a month, with unique angled ceilings, a cozy living room, and an old-fashioned kitchen. Oh, and Lord, if it's not too much to ask, I also would like to have another clawfoot bathtub."

About ten minutes after we finished praying, Bonnie's eyes fell on a newspaper ad.

"How did you miss this one, Mark?"

My heart raced as I read the ad: "Renting- an attic apartment on Ouray Avenue in Grand Junction, Colorado, for $175 a month."

It lay near the college, which added to my intrigue. We laughed in amazement and wasted no time arranging a visit. Strangely, Bonnie didn't act as surprised as I did.

We arrived at a bright yellow Victorian house with pristine white trim. The landlord greeted us with a cheerful smile, and the scent of fresh-cut grass lingered in the air. He led us up a steep flight of stairs, each step filled with excitement.

When we stepped inside, the familiar charm of the angled ceiling, a cozy living room, and a quaint kitchen welcomed us. My heart, full of amazement, pounded with anticipation as I moved toward the bathroom, holding my breath.

I turned the knob and pushed the creaky door open. There it stood—the clawfoot bathtub, glistening as if it had waited just for me—a thrill shot through me, and a wave of overwhelming joy and gratitude filled my heart. I wept as I considered the goodness of my Heavenly Father.

"Any questions now?" Bonnie quipped, her voice tinged with joy and a satisfying grin.

"No," I responded, my voice choked with emotion. "None at all."

"Thank you, Father," she whispered, lifting her hands toward heaven.

That day, I learned a profound lesson about the power of specific prayer. While I have countless stories of God's interventions, this one stands out. From healing to provision, I have seen God's hand at work in my life in numerous ways. Please don't misunderstand. I am not suggesting that God acts as a genie in a bottle granting wishes. Still, He does answer prayers, often in ways beyond our expectations.

If you desire to see the Almighty work the same way in your life, I encourage you to pray with specificity. Suppose you are seeking a life partner, for example. Detail the qualities you want and need.

Do you need a new car? Pray with exact specifications, and trust that your Father in Heaven rewards childlike trust and specific prayer requests.

Friend, as you read the following chapters, you will find more stories of the Lord's remarkable responses to specific petitions.

In closing this chapter, allow me to give a footnote: These miraculous answers to prayer do not result from our great faith. Instead, they stem from simple faith in a great God.

The Widows Home

The second Clawfoot bathtub

The Answer to Prayer

Takeaways and Lessons Learned:

1. **Trusting in God's Past Performance:** The phrase "I can trust God for my future, based upon His performance in my past" reflects a deep understanding of God's faithfulness throughout one's life. Reflect on moments in your life where God has answered prayers or provided in miraculous ways. Use these experiences as a foundation for your current and future prayers, knowing that God's track record of faithfulness gives you confidence in approaching Him with specific requests.
2. **Believing You Have Received:** This event highlights the principle that specific and detailed prayers are not presumptuous, but rather a demonstration of faith in a loving and caring God who desires to bless His children uniquely. Reflect on your own prayer life and consider if you could be more specific in your requests to God, trusting that He cares about even the most minor details of your life.

Reflection Questions for Application:

1. How did faith in God's ability to answer specific prayers play a significant role in the outcome of the situation? Consider how your faith impacts your prayers. Are there areas where you might be holding back in making specific requests to God because you fear they might be too much to ask? Embrace the belief that God can do the impossible and wants to bless you abundantly.
2. How can the principle of trusting God's performance in the past apply to your life currently? Write this in your own words.

9

The Spectacle of the Spectacles and the Lost Wallet

A Hilarious Hayfield Quest

In the middle of a sprawling 75-acre alfalfa field, Bill Bryan, my spiritual father, faced quite a predicament. Dedicated to servanthood, he spent two days on a hay baler in this vast sea of green, doing a favor for a friend.

The tractor's rumble created a background symphony to the scent of fresh-cut alfalfa under the sun's relentless gaze. After the first grueling day, he stumbled home to find his essential eyeglasses were gone.

These were not your ordinary spectacles; they were his lifeline. Without them, he was like a blind man in a dark room searching for a black cat that wasn't there.

The timing couldn't have been worse; he needed them for the Sunday sermon—study, preparation, and delivery.

Panic threatened to surge, but with a deep breath, inhaling the earthy aroma of the hayfield, he did not let fear dominate his thoughts; instead, he trusted the creator to help him find his specs.

The fresh-cut field stretched beyond him, as immense as the Texas sky. If anyone witnessed that scene, they would have laughed at the impossibility of finding a tiny pair of glasses in such an expanse. It would be like searching for a whisker on a mouse in a pile of hay, the size of Mount Everest!

Yet, Brother Bill possessed something better than doubt and fear—"Godfidence," a faith that moves mountains. He believed his Heavenly Father cared about even the most minor details of his life.

The angels above must have chuckled as he began his divine treasure hunt. The sun cast long shadows, and the fresh-cut grassy scent was potent.

The search began, and he strolled about four rows over as if guided by an unseen hand. And there they lay! His beloved spectacles glistened, nestled in the piled hay. The field seemed to rearrange itself to honor the God of the impossible, leaving us in awe of the miraculous discovery.

"Hey, Partner, come here!" Bill shouted, his voice joyful.

"You are not going to believe this!" He said, pointing.

"My glasses! Right here in the hay!"

"You've got to be kidding me," I said, shaking my head in amazement.

"Brother, let's kneel here and give thanks for this small but monumental blessing," Bill suggested.

We knelt, the hay prickling our knees. Bill started, "Lord, we are so grateful for Your guidance. Thank You for helping us find these lenses."

"Thank You, Father, for always looking out for us, even in the little things. This answer to prayer is a miracle, and we give you the glory," I added.

When we opened our eyes, we beheld the vast, endless field stretching around us. We glanced at each other in amazement and fist-bumped. Then, we raised our fists to the sky to fist-bump our Heavenly Father.

The Case of the Wandering Wallet

A couple of weeks later, I starred in our next episode of Lost and Found. Another massive hayfield found us swathing away, and when

I patted my pocket, I froze. My wallet had disappeared. Panic lurked like a crouching panther, but I remembered Bill's example.

Instead of searching in panic, I chose to pray and thank the dear Lord, not only for the hope of finding my billfold, but also for having money in it in the first place. I decided to keep working and find it later. After I worked a few hours, we joined for a cup of coffee.

"Hey, Pard, guess what?" I shouted.

Full of curiosity, he walked over to where I was.

"My wallet jumped out of my pocket into the hayfield," I said with sheepish embarrassment.

"Well, I guess it's your turn. Remember how the Lord helped us find my specs?" Bill asked with a chuckle.

"Yes, I do. Let's pray about it."

We envisioned angels rubbing their brows and shaking their heads with a smile.

"Heavenly Father, it's me again. Thank You for always helping me when I'm tempted to be anxious. Please help me find my billfold."

"And thank You, Lord, for teaching us to rely on You in all things, large and small," Bill added.

Mounting the swather, I continued to work. About fifteen minutes later, a little brown dot caught my eye. Can it be? My heart raced as I jumped off the massive hay machine and walked towards it.

Sure enough! The little brown rascal lay winking at me like a mischievous jester hidden in the grassy maze. We couldn't help but be overjoyed and relish in the victory of finding the lost item.

Bill and I always joked that God had to assemble a Special Forces unit for us two knot-heads—the "Angelic Hayfield Squad," deployed to oversee our comical escapades.

Keystone Comedy Team: Painting the Church Belfry

On another occasion, we tackled the daunting task of painting the belfry on the old country church steeple. The first ladder fell five feet short. Common sense would have urged us to get one that reached the top, but we have yet to follow the ordinary path.

Instead, in blissful ignorance and a hazardous manner, we balanced another ladder on top of the first. My job was to use my strength to hold it in place. Bill had the bucket in his teeth as he stretched as far as possible to paint. The ladder slipped once, and he froze.

"Hey, Partner, are you sure you can hold it?" Bill asked, trembling and clinging to the steeple with his fingernails like a cat.

"You scared the pee-waddin out of me, Mark!"

"The Lord's got us, brother," I reassured him.

To this day, I am convinced that the Lord, watching from above, said,

"Uh oh! My two boys are at it again; I better call in another legion of guardian angels."

Guardian Angel Blues

After six decades of looking out for me and nine for Bill, I'm sure our guardian angels developed an anxiety disorder and took up smoking.

These stories might seem trivial, but they taught a crucial lesson to a young man still learning to navigate life in the "faith lane." The key takeaway remains simple—our Heavenly Father always takes an interest in our lives, from the tiniest detail to the grandest scheme. Nothing is insignificant to our Father in Heaven. He only asks that we seek His help in everything we do, pray with Godfidence, and wait in expectation. But don't take my word for it; read it for yourself.

Psalm 5:3- NLT

"Listen to my voice in the morning, Lord. Each morning I bring my requests to you and wait in expectation."

These stories are only a few of our escapades. The world does not have enough paper to record the rest of them, but they live on in my memory, which is also a gift from above.

The Hayfield Follies

[21]

Painting the Church Belfry (Digital depiction)

[21] Tool, D. E. (2024). Keystone Comedy Team- Painting the Church Steeple [Photograph]. Online. OpenAI. (2024). ChatGPT (4o) [Large language model]. https://chatgpt.com/c/f6aafc73-2866-4a1c-b125-8d524968f22e?model=gpt-4o

Takeaways and Lessons Learned:

1. **The Power of Faith, Prayer, and Praise**: These events remind us of the power of faith and the importance of having "Godfidence"—Learning to let go of trying to control our circumstances and having unwavering confidence in God's ability to handle our problems. When we have "Godfidence," we can face challenges and uncertainties with faith, knowing that our Heavenly Father is intimately aware of every detail, whether big or small. It reminds us to trust God's loving nature and desire to be actively present in our lives.
2. **Seeing God as a Loving Father:**
   This story reveals the significance of viewing God as a loving and compassionate Father rather than a harsh judge waiting to punish. Understanding God's nature as a loving Father transforms our relationship with Him. It fosters a more profound sense of trust, openness, and vulnerability in our prayers. Instead of fearing His judgment, we can approach Him with childlike faith, knowing He cares for us like a tender parent.
3. **Gratitude for God's Miraculous Answers:**
   These events serve as reminders to cultivate a heart of gratitude for God's miraculous answers to prayer. Recognizing His hand in even the seemingly mundane aspects of our lives deepens our appreciation for His goodness. Every answered prayer becomes a testimony of His faithfulness, reinforcing our trust in Him and encouraging us to share our experiences with others to uplift and inspire them.

10

God Picks a Mate and Family Beginnings

God's guiding hand in Bringing us together.

Join me on a journey back to 1987; a turning point in my life. As a dedicated college student immersed in my spiritual walk with the Lord, I abstained from dating, and it had been five years since I last courted a girl. This commitment was to avoid distractions and temptations.

During this time, I worked at a local grocery store, where I met Gary, the produce department manager. He was a devout Christian who would soon become a pivotal figure in my love story.

While stacking apples one morning, he caught my attention with a smile.

"Hey, Mark, how's your walk with the Lord going?" he asked with genuine interest.

"It's going well, brother; thanks for asking," I replied. "The important thing is to pray and study the Bible every day. After all, it is our anchor in life."

"You are spot on," he said.

Now, Gary was being a sneaky rascal because he and his wife, Deb, knew that there was a young woman in their church who would be a perfect match for me.

"Gary, we need to get those two together," Deb said. "But how?"

"I've got it! The Valentine's banquet!" Gary shouted with a crafty grin.

About a week later, he approached me at work.

"Hey brother, our church is having a fun Valentine's banquet this Saturday, and we would love for you to come. There will be music, games, and, of course, a lot of delicious food," he added with a chuckle.

"Thank you, partner, but I'm not dating anyone, and I would feel as out of place as a banana in a peach orchard."

"That's okay, Mark. We will just be glad to have you, and other single people will be present."

Now folks, I was born at night, but not last night, and I sensed that they were plotting a matchmaking scheme. This event, orchestrated by Gary and Deb, became a peculiar twist in my disciplined path. Still, I couldn't shake the perception that the Holy Spirit had directed their invitation and might be leading me to the woman who would soon capture my heart.

The evening unfolded with heartfelt testimonies from anyone who desired to share their faith and tell everyone how they came to know Jesus as their savior.

There was no way I could be silent, so I rose to speak, lost in praise and unaware of the captivating woman in the room who would soon capture my attention. When she rose to share her life testimony, I could not help but notice her beauty, gentle spirit, and genuine passion for God.

After this inspirational event, I was near the refreshments when Ann came and stood beside me at the table.

"Hi, I'm Ann," she exclaimed with confidence and extended her hand with a warm smile.

"Mark," I replied, shaking her hand.

"Your words were inspiring tonight," she said.

"Thank you. It is always a blessing to have the opportunity to speak about the goodness of the Lord in our lives. Your testimony was uplifting as well, Ann."

"Thank you," she responded.

Our conversation revealed a deep connection, a shared love for the Bible, and a burning desire to live in complete surrender to Jesus. This divine encounter left me pondering if she might be the one my Heavenly Father had prepared for me—a partner in faith and life.

Later, I became a little confused when it appeared that Ann had come with another gentleman. True to form, crafty Gary stepped in and asked me if I would give them a ride home because Ann's car had broken down.

It seemed strange to me that Gary wouldn't take them himself. However, I agreed, and as fate would have it, I dropped her friend off first. The intensity of my attraction to her outer and inner beauty couldn't be denied as I drove to her apartment.

"Thank you for the lift," she said as we arrived at her flat. "Oh, In case you were wondering, my friend and I are just that—friends."

A spark of hope arose, and I smiled.

"That's a relief; perhaps we can meet again sometime?"

"That would be wonderful," she replied, eyes locked in mine.

"Can this be the Lord's will for me?" I pondered. The emotion was so strong that I began seeking a sign like Gideon in the Old Testament.

"Heavenly Father, please guide me. I am asking You for explicit confirmation. If I am meant to pursue this relationship, grant us an **unplanned** reconnection within the next five days. If not, let our paths remain apart."

The following day, a knock came at my door. Opening it, I was surprised to find Ann standing on the porch, radiant as a gift from Heaven.

"Hi," she said, smiling. "Since I am in the neighborhood, I thought I'd drop by and say hi."

My heart soared. The Lord orchestrated this moment; that was clear.

Because we knew this to be a divine plan, we took it day by day. Our courtship flourished over three months and exuded old-fashioned chivalry and charm. We sometimes met to delve into the Bible, discuss its wisdom, and offer frequent prayers for each other, deepening our connection. Companionship was also enjoyed as we went on long hikes, adventures, and country drives. Communication came easily for us.

One beautiful Saturday evening, the sun dipped, casting a golden hue over a serene mountain meadow. The scent of wildflowers and honeysuckle filled the air, and birds sang their approval. Ann and I walked, holding hands and enjoying the warmth of each other's touch. Being a romantic, I led her to a picturesque spot where two beautiful streams converged.

"Darlin, I uttered, my voice trembling with emotion. Our lives are like these two streams merging into one. Together, they have a greater purpose and can accomplish more."

"Sweetheart, I believe our Heavenly Father has destined for you and me to flow together into one to impact and help more people for His glory. Do you believe that, too?"

"Mark, I have been praying about this, and yes, I sense the same thing."

"Then Ann, will you marry me?"

Tears of joy and gratitude welled up in her eyes. The cool breeze rustled the leaves, and the sound of water flowing over rocks created a peaceful symphony.

"Yes, Mark, of course I will," she whispered, her voice choked with emotion.

A short time later, we celebrated our union in a joyous ceremony attended by over two hundred people. The sweet fragrance of roses filled the sanctuary, and the soft harmony of a stringed quartet set a romantic mood.

Ann walked down the aisle in a flowing white gown, and I stood breathless at her radiance as an angel prepared for me in Heaven.

The ceremony overflowed with the warmth of candlelight, the murmur of loving words exchanged, and the joyful applause of friends and family. The taste of the wedding cake, sweet and rich, lingered in our mouths as we celebrated our union.

Gary and Deb were happy and accomplished matchmakers. When we left the church, they threw a handful of rice at us and high-fived each other. Laughing, we choked and gagged on the rice all the way to the car.

The Heavenly Shepherd brought us two sheep together—a testament to His goodness—and revealed His ability to orchestrate events beyond our comprehension.

With deep reverence for His guidance, we embraced the path before us, confident that together, we could impact and help more people for His glory than we ever could, apart. This life adventure, marked by God's providence and grace, continued to unfold, deepening our faith as we faced life's joys and challenges hand in hand.

[22]

Digital depictions

[23]

[22] Tool, D. E. (2024). Match Makers: The Valentines Banquet [Digital image]. Online. OpenAI. (2024). ChatGPT (4o) [Large language model]. https://chatgpt.com/c/b7dd579d-77b0-4696-91c7-0eb9978233e3

[23] Tool, D. E. (2024). Mark Proposes to Ann [Digital Image]. Online. OpenAI. (2024). ChatGPT (4o) [Large language model]. https://chatgpt.com/c/6e9f9c59-5844-47e1-956b-7a3b43bb83ff

Takeaways and Lessons Learned:

1. **Trusting in God's Timing:** One of the key takeaways from this life event is the importance of trusting in God's timing. Even during seasons of loneliness and uncertainty, Mark remained disciplined and focused on his spiritual journey, knowing God was preparing him for something greater. When the Lord brought Ann into his life, it was evident that His timing was perfect, and everything fell into place according to His plan.
2. **Being Open to Divine Connections:** This story highlights the significance of being open to unexpected divine connections. While Mark didn't initially pursue Ann, God orchestrated the encounter and created a unique bond. It is essential to keep an open heart and mind, recognizing that God may bring someone into our lives in unexpected ways.
3. **Seeking a Shared Faith and Purpose:** Mark and Ann's shared faith and purpose in living wholeheartedly for Jesus were the firm foundation of their relationship. When praying for a mate, seek someone with the same spiritual values and priorities. A partnership built on a shared love for God and His Word can bring strength, joy, and unity, allowing you to impact lives for God's glory together.

Reflection Questions for Application:

1. Are you lonely right now? Are you praying for the right person to come along? Be encouraged by focusing on becoming the right person rather than looking for the right person. God is preparing someone ideally suited for you right now. Trust His timing. He knows when you both are ready. Then He will make it happen; you don't have to. Pray

specifically and then wait in excited expectation. You must believe that God wants the very best for you.

2. In this story, what role did "wait in expectation" play in experiencing miraculous answers to prayer and opened doors? What are some things you are asking God for? Are you praying specifically? Are you expecting your Heavenly Father to answer?

11

Answered Prayers: The Journey to Parenthood

Diapers, Doodles, Delights, and Disciples:

Two years into our marriage, the excitement of starting a family ignited within us. But as time passed, we became disheartened—our attempts to conceive remained unfruitful. Discouragement and frustration were unwelcome companions. Some people advised us to explore basic fertility testing.

One morning, we sat at the kitchen table and watched the sunrise. A soft glow bathed the room in a warm, golden light—the scent of fresh coffee and the sound of bacon frying brightened our day. The subject of infertility drugs came up, and I turned to Ann with a playful glint in my eye.

"Can you imagine?" I said, chuckling. "With our luck, will we wind up on the front cover of Time Magazine.

"Extra, read all about it: The Brutons, a family with new Octuplets!" Ann laughed, her eyes crinkling at the corners.

"We will be famous! 'The Miracle Family!'"

Laughter filled the room; a sweet melody that bounced off the walls. But beneath the humor, we both sensed a deeper purpose.

That same morning, while we immersed ourselves in prayer and Bible reading, the Lord unveiled His plan. The sun filtered through the sheer curtains, and a delicate breeze blew across the room. The pages of our Bibles rustled as we turned them, the scent of aged paper and ink rising in the stillness.

"Honey, I think we have been relying too much on science," Ann whispered, her voice filled with conviction. "We must trust the Lord more and stand firm on His promises." Her words resonated within me, and I nodded in agreement.

"It's not that we're against scientific or medical methods," I said, "but I believe our Heavenly Father is creating a different path for us."

While we read, two Bible verses leapt from the pages, reminding us of His faithfulness throughout history. **Genesis 25:21** portrayed how Isaac prayed for his barren wife, and God, in boundless mercy, answered with Rebekah's conception. In **Psalms 113:9**, our hearts rejoiced as we read about Divine intervention granting families to the childless, bringing happiness and fulfillment.

The story of Abraham and Sarah's improbable journey to parenthood in their old age also brought encouragement and laughter to our hearts. I imagined a 100-year-old Abraham, shuffling into the room with the earthy scent of old wood as he sipped his tea from a saucer, his eyes full of mischief. Abraham glanced at 90-year-old Sarah snoring away in her rocking chair with a smelly old cat on her lap and her mouth agape.

"Hey baby," he said, his voice soft and husky. "The Lord told me we are going to have a baby."

Picture the scene, if you will: Sarah spits her dentures out in laughter, which creates a vibe that fills the room with her doubt. Nine months later, God's promise came true, making them the only couple to pay for their pediatrician with a social security check.

Inspired by these tales of God's miraculous provision, in 1988, we began to pray, declare, and stand firm on His promises. The Lord, in His infinite goodness, did not disappoint. In 1989, our firstborn son, Isaac, graced our lives. True to his name, he always brought laughter, wit, and endless joy to our family. Now, he is a businessman. However, I have always thought that he would be a dynamo of a comedian. Isaac is blessed with two beautiful children: Channy and Liam.

Then, in 1991, God gifted us with a second child. Jacob, a fearless adventurer who always perched himself atop tall trees, with rough bark scratching and scarring him. Because of this boy, we knew the local emergency room staff by their first names. It was Jacobs's habit to capture animals with homemade traps and snares. For example, he once caught an iguana, the size of a house cat.

"Dad, look what I found… I'm going to build him a cage." And he did.

Or the time he brought a wriggly frog to the dinner table.

"Hey guys, look what I caught!" Jacob exclaimed. "I'm going to create a habitat for him in the bathtub."

"You and your adventures, Jacob," Ann said as she chuckled.

About a week later, the house smelled like a broken freezer with rotten meat. We encouraged Jacob to build his habitats in the outdoors.

Mud, dirt, grass, and the scent of the outdoors accompany him to this day. Jacob always built things and worked hard with his hands. Now in his thirties, he and his wife Kinsey have two fantastic boys. He owns a multi-million-dollar construction company in Gunnison and Crested Butte, Colorado.

In 1993, the arrival of the darling of our souls, Rebekah, captured our hearts. Her big brown eyes and lashes that could double for wings wrapped her daddy around her little finger from the start and still do thirty-one years later.

"No, Becky."

"But, Daddy, blink, blink, blink…"

It is incredible how this still works on me every time.

Becky is an admirable mother of three: Jaycee, Trace, and Lexee. After being a stay-at-home mom for years, she completed her educator training and is now a popular teacher.

Allow me to digress a little. With the responsibility of nurturing our children's physical, emotional, and spiritual needs, we vowed to God and each other to adhere to His principles found in the Bible. We aimed to teach them the value of a close, one-on-one relationship with the Heavenly Father.

Through laughter and tears, faith, and trust in the Almighty, we cherished the precious blessing of family. The smell of fresh-baked cookies and laughter reminded us daily of God's goodness and still lingers in our memories. This beautiful journey passed way too fast. However, a few days during their adolescence made us understand why some animals eat their young.

God blessed us with three unique children and seven incredible grandchildren. It is my prayer that this humble work blesses many. But I have written this book especially for them. The following pages will recount more stories of how He answered specific family prayers, demonstrating to our children that God is real, not just a Sunday school story.

[24]

Take fertility drugs, or trust the Lord?

---

[24] Tool, D. E. (2024). Mark and Ann with quintuplets [Digital image]. Online. OpenAI. (2024). ChatGPT (4o) [Large language model]. https://chatgpt.com/c/b7dd579d-77b0-4696-91c7-0eb9978233e3

 [25]

Trust the Lord (Digital Depiction)

Takeaways and Lessons Learned:

1. **Trust in God's Timing and Plan**: Mark and Ann's journey to parenthood taught them the importance of trusting in God's timing and plan, even when it differed from their own. The frustration and discouragement they faced while trying to conceive reminded them that they must rely on God and His promises. Take a few moments and reflect on the Bible verses that encouraged the Brutons:
    - Genesis 25:21: Isaac's prayer for Rebekah's barrenness and God's merciful response.
    - Psalms 113:9: God's intervention in granting families to the childless.

[25] Tool, D. E. (2024). Mark and Ann buy their first home [Digital image]. Online. OpenAI. (2024). ChatGPT (4o) [Large language model]. https://chatgpt.com/c/b7dd579d-77b0-4696-91c7-0eb9978233e3

Reflection Questions for Application:

1. When facing challenges or delays in life, remember that God has a plan for you. Lean on His promises, seek His guidance in prayer, and trust He will provide in His perfect timing.

The Power of Faith and Prayer

2. The author's story highlights the power of faith and prayer. When they decided to rely less on human methods and more on God's promises, they experienced His miraculous provision. Their prayers, coupled with child-like faith, led to the births of three unique children.
3. Make prayer and faith central to your daily life. In difficult situations, immerse yourself in prayer and stand firm on God's promises and declare them out loud. Trust that He hears your prayers and will act according to His will.

Embrace the Unique Journey of Parenthood

4. Raising their children—Isaac, Jacob, and Rebekah—taught them to cherish the journey of parenthood with its ups and downs. Each child brought their unique personality, challenges, and joys, and spiced up the Bruton family which added flavor to life.
5. Embrace your family's unique journey, appreciating the individual traits and gifts each member brings. Nurture your relationships with love, patience, and faith, knowing God has blessed you with each person for a reason.

12

When God Turns Dreams into Reality

The Miracle on Meadowlark Lane

In 1989, my wife and I rented an old-fashioned, charming, quaint Italian cottage that had journeyed across oceans to settle on American soil.

This cozy two-bedroom home, with its creaking cherry wood floors, the scent of old pine, unique cabinets, and a front porch with a swing, is a testament to God's providence. Its modest monthly rent of $225 was also a blessing.

At that time, I found myself in a unique situation. Despite my education and BA degree in teaching, I sensed a strong pull from the Holy Spirit to learn a new trade— that of a meat cutter in a prominent grocery store. This unexpected turn was a clear sign of divine guidance in my life; it was a lucrative profession with great benefits.

At the same time, after much prayer and counsel, I decided to relinquish my role as pastor of the congregation I'd led for three years.

After searching, the church hired a minister, and I transferred to Ann's Bible-based New Testament congregation, governed by a plurality of elders. Later, I became one of the elders responsible for speaking on Sundays.

"Do you mean to say you joined the Mormons?" You ask.

"No, I did not."

This group of dear people followed the New Testament principles of governance. None of us received a salary from the ministry; we all sustained ourselves through our occupations.

This structure mirrored the Biblical model and freed me from shouldering the responsibility alone. This group of overseers operates as a cohesive pastoral team so that they can address the congregation's needs in a more complete manner.

This approach aligned with what I believe is God's original intent for assembling His children (See Acts 2:42).

Our members devoted themselves to studying the Bible and praying, echoing A.W. Tozer's sentiment:

"It is better to be in a small church where God is big than in a big church where God is small."

The Bruton family grew with the arrival of our firstborn, Isaac. The cozy little cottage became cramped, and we often talked about our dream home.

"Mark, imagine a rustic house with three bedrooms, two baths, and a moss-rock fireplace," Ann said, her eyes full of hope.

I nodded and smiled at the thought.

"Let's pray for those specifics, sweetheart, and that the Lord will provide them without debt."

"That will take a miracle!" she exclaimed.

"Exactly," I replied, remembering His faithfulness in the past. "He is the God of the impossible," I continued.

Every day, we thanked our Heavenly Father for what he would do in our lives.

To digress, a year before this heartfelt prayer, we experienced the passing of Grandma Bruton, a prosperous and influential businesswoman who managed Bruton's Conoco for over five decades. Granny always wished for my brother and me to continue the family legacy. However, I sensed the Holy Spirit guiding me in a different direction for a higher purpose.

My brother and I knew that leaving the family business meant forfeiting any inheritance or residual income from the profitable enterprise. However, I found complete peace in my decision, knowing it was in alignment with the Lord's will for my life. This peace and conviction in God's plan were a testament to my faith.

Now, let's go back to when we were praying for a debt-free home. On one eventful Wednesday, while engrossed in my duties at the store, Anna appeared, holding an envelope from an attorney's office—her face, pale with worry.

"Mark, what do you think this is?" she asked, her voice trembling.

Anxiety gripped us like facing a snarling dragon that emerged from a dark cave.

"Not sure, honey. Are we in legal trouble? Did we wrong someone, and now we face a lawsuit?" Taking the envelope from her, my hands began to tremble.

A truth emerged as we unfolded the letter filled with cryptic legalese.

"Ann, I can't believe it. We are beneficiaries of the Bernice Bruton estate. We've inherited $50,000!"

Ann's eyes widened in joy.

"This is incredible! This money is God's miraculous provision that we have prayed for."

The new house we found and asked for cost $45,000 (remember, it was 1989). With the contract signed and secured, we paid the entire sum at closing with a cashier's check from our inheritance in three weeks. This windfall enabled us to buy our home and left us with $5,000 to furnish it. Our hearts brimmed with gratitude, and we praised our Heavenly Father for His miraculous provision.

"Can you believe this?" my wife said as we stepped across the threshold of our new abode.

The sun's warmth filtered through the windows and shone down on the rustic wooden walls and the moss-rock fireplace with a vast bridge timber mantle—just what we asked for.

"It's perfect, Ann; more than we could have ever imagined," I replied as I wrapped her in my arms.

Gratitude filled our hearts for Grandma Bruton in heaven, who remembered me in her will even after I departed from the family business. The gesture reminded us that the divine plan always surpasses our limited understanding.

Filled with joy and exhilaration, we settled into our new home, a haven for the arrival of two more cherished additions to our family. This home provided the perfect place for us, a fresh new start and boundless dreams.

Yet, unknown to us, the Almighty created another extraordinary plan and held it in the wings, a mutual life-long dream etched in our souls since we were young.

This anticipation of His next miraculous move held us in rapt anticipation, perched on the edge of our seats, because we knew the Lord would grace us with even more blessings. Before I delve into that remarkable tale, I must share a cherished memory with you in the next chapter.

[26]

Digital depiction

[26] Tool, D. E. (2024). Mark and Ann buy their first home [Digital image]. Online. OpenAI. (2024). ChatGPT (4o) [Large language model]. https://chatgpt.com/c/b7dd579d-77b0-4696-91c7-0eb9978233e3

Takeaways and Lessons Learned:

1. **Trust in God's Timing and Provision:** The author's story illustrates the importance of trusting God's timing and provision. Despite initial uncertainties and fears, the unexpected inheritance was a clear example of how God provides in miraculous ways, reinforcing the belief that God is always in control and knows our needs better than we do.
2. **Power of Persistent Prayer:** The consistent and heartfelt prayers for a specific home were answered in an extraordinary manner. This teaches us the power of persistent and specific prayer, showing that God listens to our desires and can answer them in ways that exceed our expectations.
3. **Following God's Guidance over Personal Plans:** The author's decision to follow God's calling, even when it meant leaving a lucrative family business, underscores the lesson that God's plans are higher than ours. The peace and fulfilment found in following God's direction affirm that true satisfaction comes from obedience to His will.

Reflection Questions for Application:

1. **How Can I Trust God's Provision in My Current Situation?**
   - Reflect on a current need or desire in your life. How can you trust in God's timing and provision for this situation? Consider ways to deepen your faith and patience, knowing that God understands your needs and has a plan for you.
2. **What Specific Prayers do I Need to Bring Before God?**
   - Think about the dreams and desires you have for your life. How can you bring these to God in prayer with persistence and faith? Reflect on the importance of being

specific in your prayers and trusting that God hears and answers in His perfect timing.

3. **Where is God Calling Me to Follow His Guidance Over My Plans?**
    - o Examine areas in your life where you might be holding on to your own plans rather than seeking God's guidance. How can you open yourself to His direction, even if it means making complex or unexpected changes? Reflect on the peace that comes from trusting in God's higher purpose for your life.

13

The Little Tykes Playhouse Miracle

How God Answered Little Hearts' Prayers

In the summer of 1995, unbeknownst to us, our family was headed for a faith adventure at Walmart that would leave an indelible impression on all of us. We stepped through the store's sliding doors, and the cool, air-conditioned breeze hit our faces, a welcome relief from the sweltering heat.

The fluorescent lights overhead buzzed and illuminated aisles that brimmed with vibrant merchandise. Our excited kids, with eyes full of wonder, giggled as they spotted the Little Tykes' multi-colored climbing playhouse. Its bright, primary colors and sturdy plastic structure beckoned them like buried treasure.

"Daddy, look at this! Can we have it, please?" they pleaded, with Becky batting her eyelashes in her usual way.

I almost spit Coca-Cola out my nostrils when I noticed the $185 price tag. "Sorry, kids, we can't afford it right now."

Their spirits remained undampened. They climbed and played with boundless delight. Their laughter echoed through the store until their faces flushed and their hair matted with sweat.

After shopping, we prepared to leave, and I reminded them, "It breaks my heart, kiddos, but we can't buy it today."

Their disappointed countenance tugged at our heartstrings; their eyes reflected a mix of understanding and longing. The goal was to be wise with our finances, but I felt lower than a snake's belly in a wagon rut.

After we all hopped into the family van, an idea sparked, and I am sure I resembled Wiley E. Coyote with a lightbulb over his head.

"This will be a perfect teachable moment for trusting God and the value of specific prayer," I whispered to Ann.

"Hey, kids," I said. "How about we pray and ask our Heavenly Father for a Jungle gym like that one?"

Their eyes lit up at the thought, and we prayed together. Dad led off, followed by Momma and each child, offering heartfelt prayers as they hoped for divine intervention.

The kids misunderstood the purpose of our petition because they thought that saying "amen" meant they could dash back into the store at that moment and claim the playset as theirs.

"Hold on, youngsters! When we pray, we ask and then wait for His answer."

On our way home, a random thought crossed my mind, and I decided to take a different, seldom-traveled route through the back entrance of our subdivision. Little did I know that this impromptu decision would lead to a miraculous twist of fate—a turn of events that would leave us all in awe.

We turned into Meadowlark Lane, and there it sat! A Little Tykes playset stood proud in someone's yard, looking brand new!

The kids hadn't seen it yet, so I stopped, backed out of eyeshot, and parked the car. Filled with enthusiasm, I walked to the house, glanced upward, and whispered, "Lord, this is just like you!" An older gentleman greeted me at the door, his face etched with years of kindness.

"Excuse me, sir, this is an odd question from a stranger, but would you be interested in selling that playset?" His reply brought tears to my eyes.

"Well, funny you should ask; our grandkids moved away, and now we don't have much use for the colorful contraption. We plan to sell it at our yard sale tomorrow."

"How much will you ask for it, sir?"

"Would $25 be fair?"

Trying to suppress my delight, I assured them the price was fair. The kind neighbors agreed to sell it to us, and I wanted to shout with joy as I rushed back to the van. I couldn't contain my excitement.

"Well?" Ann asked.

"We got it for $25 bucks!" I murmured with a grin on my face.

With ecstatic hearts, I drove forward and pointed, "Hey, kids, what do you see?" The miracle unfolded; the exact playhouse they had asked for was smiling at them!

"Daddy! It is a jungle gym, just like the one we prayed for."

"It's yours!" I spoke.

"Yay, He did it! Jesus gave us the playhouse!" The kids cheered.

The youngins realized their prayer requests were granted, and their trust was bolstered, which thrilled us to our core.

"Can you believe this? God answered our prayer and has shown us that He has a great sense of humor!" Ann said.

"The Lord won't always act that fast, guys, but the principle is always the same: pray, trust, wait, and praise," I said, trying to add balance to the situation.

Giggles filled the air as we took it apart and loaded it into the vehicle. The children couldn't believe what had happened, and we marveled at how He had brought us on this wild spiritual journey.

That day, our kiddos learned a valuable lesson—that God loves us, wants us to ask Him, and He hears and longs to answer our prayers. We, as parents, also learned the importance of teaching our children to trust in God's timing and to be patient in waiting for His answers.

Together, our family discovered the magic of trusting our Creator with our deepest desires, with a dash of laughter and abundant love.

The memory of that day still fills our hearts with gratitude, and we will forever cherish when God's love and grace led us from the aisles of Wal-Mart to a random neighbor's backyard. Our hearts overflowed with joy and gratitude for this divine intervention.

[27]

Bruton, M. W. (2024). Little Tykes Playset [Photograph]. Personal Photos.

Takeaways and Lessons Learned:

1. **The Power of Specific Prayer**: The chapter highlights the importance of being specific in our prayers. By asking God for specific needs and desires, such as the exact playhouse the children wanted, we can see His hand at work more clearly when those prayers are answered. This specificity strengthens our faith and helps us recognize God's direct intervention in our lives.
2. **Teaching Children to Trust in God**: The author used the opportunity to teach his children about faith and trust in God. This lesson was not just about asking for things but

27

understanding that God hears our prayers and responds in His perfect timing. This experience taught the children that they could rely on God for their needs and desires, fostering a lifelong habit of prayer and trust.

3. **God's Unexpected Blessings**: The miraculous provision of the playhouse reminds us that God can provide for our needs and desires in the most unexpected ways. This teaches us to remain open and expectant, knowing that God's solutions often come from places we least anticipate. It encourages us to trust that God's plans are always better and more creative than ours.

Reflection Questions for Application:

1. **How Can I Incorporate Specific Prayers in My Daily Life?**
   - Reflect on your current prayer life. How often do you pray specifically for your needs and desires? Consider setting aside time daily to bring detailed requests before God, trusting that He hears and answers them according to His perfect will.
2. **How Am I Teaching the Next Generation to Trust in God?**
   - Think about how you impart faith and trust in God to the children in your life, whether they are your children, grandchildren, or others. How can you create more opportunities to teach them about God's faithfulness and encourage them to rely on Him through prayer and trust?
3. **When Have I Experienced God's Unexpected Blessings?**
   - Reflect on a time when God provided for you in an unexpected way. How did this experience impact your faith? Consider journaling about these moments to remind yourself of God's faithfulness and to encourage you to trust Him more deeply in future challenges and desires.

14

Blessed Acres

God's Hand in Bringing Us to Our Little Farm

In a quaint corner of God's intricate plan, our family nestled into our cozy home on Meadowlark Lane, and we savored all of the joys life had bestowed upon us.

After we lived in our house for three years, Ann and I longed for the simplicity of country life, a shared dream—a place where our children could have animals, chores, and responsibilities, and we could be more self-sufficient.

Still, we were content with the small subdivision God provided for us. Little did we know that a life change awaited us right around the corner, a change that would stir our hearts and test our faith in ways we could never have imagined.

Wanting to expose our kids to ranch life, we took them to the Moon Farm in Fruita, Colorado, on a Saturday. When we arrived, the scent of hay and livestock lingered.

The place buzzed with enchantment and adventure as children laughed on pony rides, ran among sculpted dinosaurs, and played with an array of animals—sheep bleated, lambs scampered, goats nibbled, cows mooed, pigs snorted, ducks quacked, geese honked, and chickens clucked. Our hearts danced with dreams of a mini farmstead to call our own. After a long day of play and adventures, we headed home.

"Daddy, I wish we could have some cows, pigs, lambs, and chickens," a dreamy voice piped up from the backseat.

"Me too, guys," I replied, imagining a little ranch where they could care for their critters.

"We should pray about it, Dad, just like we did with the playset," Isaac, our eldest son, suggested in child-like faith.

Our children's innocence and faith shone brightly, filling us with joy and hope. Their simple belief in the power of prayer prompted a roadside pause. Ann and I exchanged glances, excitement and anticipation gleaming in our eyes. Could this be a new path charted by our Father in Heaven?

As we prayed, the children shared their specific desires. They voiced requests for the animals they wanted and envisioned in their dreams. Pure joy and hope filled the moment, and each heartbeat echoed the suspense of the Lord's response and the miraculous revelation of our prayers.

That evening, Ann and I, fueled by hopefulness, pondered the prospect of the Lord gracing our family with a little mini ranch. Could this be the divine convergence of dreams and reality? We envisioned raising our children in an environment of hard work and responsibility, surrounded by the rustic charm of life in the country.

About a month later, fate guided Ann and me down a back road in Clifton, Colorado, after a routine errand. Traffic was backed up ahead, and our curiosity peaked. What spectacle lay beyond the congestion?

Our eyes turned to the right, and there it stood—a captivating old blue-white-trimmed farmhouse adorned with a tire swing and an old-fashioned porch that whispered of simpler times, like a nostalgic Norman Rockwell painting.

"No wonder everyone is driving so slowly. Look!" I exclaimed.

Cows, pigs, goats, chickens, and ducks grazed freely in the front yard of this sentimental lot, which caused traffic to back up. The charm of the sight enthralled everyone.

Yet, the **for-sale-by-owner** sign, standing sentinel on a five-acre canvas, seized our attention. Could this be the answer to our fervent prayers? Excitement kindled as we headed homeward, prepared to lay our specific requests before our Heavenly Father and seek His will and financial guidance.

The call to the listed number connected us with a knowledgeable lady who owned the century-old farmhouse. The asking price of $65,000 was within reach, and we envisioned modest additions and upgrades amounting to $20,000.

Our faith, a constant companion, guided us as we prepared to sell our home. With collective trust in God's providence, we embarked on this uncharted odyssey, and we consulted, prayed with, and involved our kids in every step of the discourse. Our faith was not just a belief but a living, breathing force that shaped our decisions and sustained us through the uncertainties of this journey.

On an evening drive to see the farm, our children were filled with wonder at the pastoral scene—a miniature Noah's Ark with critters of all kinds roaming free. The scent of hay and the earthy aroma of animals mingled with the cool evening breeze as we enveloped this potential homestead; our prayers ascended, specific and sincere.

Anticipation, thick as the morning mist, hung in the air as we awaited divine guidance. Would this be where our prayers transformed into tangible reality, a testament to God's miraculous provision? The next few days unfolded a faith journey filled with hope and a deep reliance on God's timing and plan.

In a whirlwind of divine orchestration, our home was purchased for $45,000 three years prior. The yard now displayed a **for-sale-by-owner** signpost that beckoned $65,000. As I planted the small billboard in our yard, the neighbor across the street had a realtor showing their house simultaneously.

After showing their house, the pompous realtor strutted over, presented his business card, and dismissed by-owner sales as ineffective. He spouted statistics, reiterated his doubt, and warned us that selling a house without professional help invites frustration. Yet, Godfidence anchored us.

Within thirty minutes of planting the sign, an unexpected call came. The lady looking at the neighbor's house with the real estate agent called and requested to see our home.

"Hello, I was in the neighborhood today looking at houses and saw your sign. I would love to see it. I won't bring the agent because you are selling it by owner."

"Thank you. You are more than welcome to come and see it. We have nothing against brokers but are trying to save money on that expense."

When she stepped into our quaint abode, excitement overtook her.

"Oh my gosh! This is the house I have been searching for six months! "Can you take $58,000?" she asked. "I am pre-approved for that amount."

The sum fell short of our asking price. Firm in our conviction, we stayed with our Heavenly Father's plan.

I'm sorry, Ma'am. It has been appraised at $65,000. We can't let it go for less. Do you think your bank will approve you for more?"

The woman did not negotiate further but said, "I will go to my bank tomorrow."

The Lord worked another miracle: she secured the money within a day, which gave us $20,000 more than its initial purchase price three years prior. Because our home was paid off, we had the exact amount to buy the little ranch.

With our place sold, we ventured forward and placed a contract on the farmhouse tethered to the sale of our previous home. Guided by the gracious lady who owned the little ranch, paperwork unfolded seamlessly, a testament to God's meticulous care over the details.

Excitement hit a crescendo as we prepared to move—the prospect of a dream mini-farm tangible on the horizon.

After we settled into our quaint and rustic little farmhouse, we witnessed the miracle created by prayer and divine provision. The rhythm of life in the country—a symphony of demanding work and fulfillment—unfolded before us. A Hereford cow and a calf marked the start of our journey, and alongside them, three pigs—Ham, Porkchop, and Bacon—each embodying a purpose beyond mere companionship.

Our children, hands in the soil, learned the nuances of responsibility as they helped build fences, mend corrals, fill water troughs, milk goats, gather eggs, and tend to the animals. Life on our little rancho brimmed with purpose and divine grace.

Every resource the farm offered—eggs, beef, pork, and milk—provided for us and amplified our sense of self-sufficiency. We bred pygmy goats, sold them, and marveled as our children observed new life entering the world.

As we reveled in the joy of country life, we couldn't help but reflect on the journey. How specific prayers met divine answers and God's faithfulness as our continual guide. The idyllic scene, painted with gratitude and joy, is once again, a living testament to God's goodness.

In a funny twist of fate, a month into our new refuge, I bumped into the skeptical and arrogant realtor who had scoffed at our decision to sell by owner. I shared our story with a satisfied smile—how the house sold in under an hour, and the little ranch was now ours. I wanted to ask him if he wished to have my card, but humility restrained me. The Father above orchestrated the encounter; a chuckle from above at the irony of doubt turned to triumph.

Many memories are etched on that farm, like the rich scent of fresh-cut hay and the feel of dirt under our nails. Children's laughter echoed through the fields, and the taste of homegrown produce, milk, meat, and eggs became the pillars of gratitude in our lives.

God's love and guidance resonated through every step, evidence of a Heavenly Father who delights in blessing His children. Our children are still grateful for the answer to our prayer and for a farm to grow up on. May the Almighty be praised!

The Boys on our little farm 1995

The Boys playing on
their favorite log.
1994

Jacob and Isaac

28

Takeaways and Lessons Learned:

1. **The Power of Specific and Faithful Prayer**: The author's story underscores the importance of praying with specificity

[28] Bruton, M. W. (2024). Kids on the farm [Photograph]. Personal Photos.

and faith. The family witnessed God's precise and miraculous answers by involving the children in praying for a farm with particular features. This teaches us to approach God with detailed requests and trust that He hears and responds to our needs and desires.

2. **Trust in God's Timing and Plan:** The narrative reveals the significance of trusting God's perfect timing and plan. Despite initial setbacks and uncertainties, the author's unwavering faith in God's provision resulted in the family finding and acquiring their dream farm. This demonstrates that God's plans often unfold in unexpected ways but always align with His greater purpose for our lives.
3. **Embracing Opportunities for Faith Lessons:** Mark and Ann used the experience as a teaching moment for their children, reinforcing the values of prayer, patience, and trust in God. This highlights the importance of seizing opportunities to impart spiritual lessons to the next generation, helping them develop a strong foundation of faith.

Reflection Questions for Application:

1. **How Can I Make My Prayers More Specific and Faith-Filled?**
   - Reflect on your current prayer life. How can you incorporate more specific and faith-filled requests in your prayers? Consider setting aside time to clearly articulate your needs and desires to God, trusting that He will answer in His perfect timing.

2. **In What Areas do I need to Trust God's Timing and Plan?**
   - Think about situations in your life where you may struggle to trust God's timing and plan. How can you surrender these areas to Him and rely on His guidance?

Reflect on past experiences where God's timing proved perfect, and let those memories strengthen your faith.

3. **How Can I Use My Experiences to Teach Others About Faith?**
   - Consider the opportunities to share your faith journey with others, especially younger generations. How can you use your experiences of God's provision and guidance to teach and inspire them? Reflect on practical ways to incorporate faith lessons into everyday life and conversations.

15

Miracle on Wheels: The Blue ASTRO VAN

Beyond Expectations: A Tale of Faith and Answered Prayer

Before moving to the farm, I drove a Volkswagen Beetle, which I called my "pregnant roller skate." The VW was unsuitable for ranch life, so the Lord provided a solution through a man who owned a truck but wanted a Volkswagen Bug. We traded straight across and thanked God for the provision of a rugged vehicle more suitable for work.

The truck was great for ranch work, but as our family grew, so did our need for a larger car. With five people, we now needed a spacious, reliable, and safe vehicle. Some friends of ours owned a brown Astro van, which sparked our desire for a similar one.

The Bible instructs in **1 John 5:15 and Philippians 4:6** not to worry about anything, but to pray specifically about everything. Therefore, we prayed for a metallic blue Astro van with low mileage, between 30,000 and 40,000 miles, priced at $7,000, which we could pay for in cash from our savings and avoid debt.

Many doubted our Godfidence. "Mark," they asked, "isn't it presumptuous to put specifics on God like that? And isn't it impossible and borderline heresy to expect such precise results?"

These dear friends were unaware that we had witnessed our Heavenly Father accomplish the impossible countless times before, and this time would be no different.

As a family, we knelt around the piano bench, feeling the softness of the carpet beneath our knees and the warmth of each other's presence. Together, we asked our Father in Heaven for our new family ride, united in our faith and shared prayer.

"Heavenly Father, you know our need. We want to ask you for a blue Chevy Astro Minivan," Ann prayed.

"Father, please give us a cool and safe car that doesn't cost Mommy and Daddy too much money," Isaac requested.

"Dear Jesus, we want a car to play in and sleep in. Can you make it big enough to bring all our friends to the park, and maybe even fit a pizza in the backseat for a snack party?" Jacob uttered.

"Hi, Jesus! It's me, Becky. I hope you're having a good day up in Heaven! We need a van. Also, can you make it blue, like my favorite blueberry ice cream?" Becky's innocent and pure prayer reminded me of the simplicity and sincerity of a child's faith.

"Oh Lord, thank you already for providing the vehicle you want us to have. Please, lead us to it, Father." I asked in deep reverence.

Soon after, we began to see Astro vans everywhere, but none matched our prayer's precise criteria. A local car dealer did have a blue Astro minivan, but there was some rust, and it had 77,000 miles and a sales tag of around $9,000.

Despite its allure, we detected an ominous sound from underneath while test-driving it. The rear axle sounded like my joints when I get up in the mornings—a loud creaking grinding sound, like I'm walking on bubble wrap.

Because it did not meet our specific prayer stipulations, we continued to trust our Lord. We believed He would lead us to the perfect car for our family.

One day, while visiting my grandmother in another town, we decided to stop by a Ford dealership on a whim, even though the Astro is a Chevy.

The car salesman pounced on us like ants on a milkshake straw. "I'll bet you are looking for a family car!" He voiced in the speed and tone of an auctioneer.

He showed us an Aerostar, but it didn't resonate with us. The dashboard seemed capable of landing a 747, and the car's body was built as if it went into a tunnel with insufficient height, peeling it like a banana.

"We want a Chevy Astro van, sir," I said with determination.

"You are aware that you are at a Ford dealership, right?" The salesman asked.

Embarrassed, we acknowledged how far-fetched it sounded, but we thought they might have gotten a trade-in.

All of a sudden, he said, "Wait a minute, folks. I just remembered something!" Lifting his walkie-talkie to his mouth, "Hey Tony, do we still have that minivan we got three days ago? What is the model of that car?"

With enthusiasm, the dealer announced, "Folks, you're not going to believe this, but we happen to have a beautiful Astro van on the wash rack right now. I am pleased to tell you that it passed our 41 multipoint safety and mechanical inspection with flying colors. They say it belonged to an older couple who had taken great care of it."

Our hearts skipped a beat. When we walked into the room, it was sitting on the rack, detailed, looking brand new, metallic **blue, and it sparkled** like a giant diamond on a bride's finger.

"That's it, Dad! The vehicle we prayed for!" Jacob squealed.

I tamed their excitement by reminding them that we still had some things to review. Our hearts beat faster than a hummingbird's wings, and we were excitedly shaking like a paint mixer.

With permission, I examined the mileage. Tears of joy rose in my eyes—33,000 miles are all it had on it, meeting another of our prayer's specific requests.

One last hurdle remained—the price. The dealer quoted $10,200, way beyond our budget of $7,000. Even though we about swallowed our teeth, we did not lose hope and remained confident that God led us to this moment.

With faith in our hearts and confidence, we offered our $7,000 for the $10,200 minivan.

"With that kind of mileage, there is no way we can let it go for that amount," remarked the salesman as he chuckled and scratched his head.

The car dealer did the usual song and dance and agreed to discuss it with his boss. We understood the negotiation tactics but stood firm in our Godfidence and trust in divine provision. Now, we realized that they would try to upsell us with an exclusive deal on Blinker fluid and muffler bearings. Our faith was being tested because we wanted THAT car!

"Ann, should we bite the bullet, pay more, and secure a small loan?"

But we reminded ourselves, "Wait! What are we thinking? God has met all our requests; the money is no problem for Him."

The sales associate returned, "The owner says he will let it go for $8,000, and this is our best offer."

We clarified that we could only negotiate up to $7,000. I engaged the salesman, my voice steady. The man looked at us in disbelief as we continued to negotiate.

"Friend, you need to sell a car, and we need a family vehicle. Both of us can walk away as winners. Most importantly, we want you to understand that we are a Christian family. We believe in the power of prayer and have prayed about this car's specifics. We believe this automobile was meant for us. $7,000 is our final proposal," I said, determined.

"Therefore, please make our last offer without the intention to dilly-dally further about the price."

The sales associate seemed doubtful but agreed to present our bid to his boss. Our family prayed in silence, the air thick with anticipation. The dealership owner glanced at us through the window several times, his expression thoughtful.

After what seemed to be an eternity, the associate returned, shaking his head in amazement. He stated that in a decade of working with this owner, he had never seen him come down in price this much on a used vehicle.

That day, the extraordinary happened—the owner agreed to our offer of $7,000. Later, we found out that he, too, was a Christian, admired our faith, and wanted to bless our family. Tears of joy streamed down our faces as we realized God intervened again and caused the man to show kindness and favor.

The cash was handed to them with pleasure and immense gratitude. We knew God's hand was present in this transaction. The entire family became as excited as a monkey on a five-mile grapevine.

With smiles, we drove off in our new shiny **blue** Chevy Astro van, which had only 33,000 miles and cost us **$7,000.** We marveled at the goodness and faithfulness of our Heavenly Father.

Our children witnessed, once again, the reality of God's presence in our lives through this miraculous answer to a specific prayer. God received all the glory for the way He orchestrated this incredible moment. Once more, it was proven that He is a loving Father who cares for His children's needs and delights in surprising them with His kindness.

Later, as the sun set with a peaceful orange and golden glow and that new car scent, we drove home and offered our heartfelt thanks to the Lord for His endless love and for answering our prayers in ways that far exceeded our expectations.

The blue minivan became more than just a vehicle. It became a tangible reminder of God's faithfulness, a testament to the power of specific prayer, and a cherished symbol of His goodness in our lives.

[29]

Our Blue Astro Van

Takeaways/Lessons Learned:

1. **The Power of Specific Prayer:** This story underscores the significance of praying with precision and detail. The family's specific requests for a metallic blue Astro van with low mileage at a particular price were miraculously answered. It reminds us that being specific in our prayers can lead to remarkable outcomes.
2. **Faith and Trust in God's Provision:** The family's unwavering faith and trust in God's provision are evident

[29] Bruton, M. W. (2024). Blue Astro Van- Digitally Enhanced [Photograph]. Personal Photos.

throughout the story. They believed God would provide exactly what they asked for, even when faced with challenges. Their confidence in divine intervention demonstrates the importance of trusting God's plan, especially in impossible situations.

3. **God's Unexpected Ways:** The family's encounter at the Ford dealership illustrates how God can work unexpectedly. Even though they were at a different dealership and the odds seemed against them, the perfect van appeared when they least expected it. This serves as a reminder that God's timing and methods often surpass human understanding, highlighting the need to remain open to unexpected opportunities.

Reflection Questions for application:

1. How can you incorporate the principle of specific prayer and declaring God's word out loud into your own life? Are there areas where you've been praying vaguely that could benefit from greater specificity?
2. Reflect on a situation in your life where you were challenged to have faith and trust in God's provision. How did your perspective change as the situation unfolded?
3. Consider a time when you experienced an unexpected turn of events that led to a positive outcome. How did this experience shape your understanding of divine intervention and the importance of remaining open to God's guidance?

16

From Minivan to Moo-van

A Cow Hauling Misadventure

There is nothing quite like springtime on a farm! Blossoms burst into color and fragrance, fresh shoots break through the soil, and adorable newborn critters prance around, reminiscent of an old Disney movie scene.

"Don't you love spring?" my son asked as he watched a group of baby lambs frolic in the field. "Everything is so alive and green, Daddy."

Being in the health and fitness industry, I have always been devoted to eating healthy food. The idea of a fattened cow never appealed to me.

"Fat-marbled beef might taste delicious," I explained to my wife, "but all that excess flab isn't healthy for the heart. Let's bypass on the triple bypass and go for a leaner breed, like Holstein."

After our research, we found that we could buy a dairy calf for fifty dollars and raise it ourselves. The kids would enjoy bottle-feeding the little critter, and a lean-breed calf would be much cheaper and more fun than a Hereford heifer.

Our journey began as we scoured the livestock ads.

"Hey, guys! There is a dairy with calves for sale about thirty miles away," I expressed, as I pointed to an ad. "The only problem is we need a livestock trailer or something to haul the critter. But who needs that when you have a trusty minivan?" I joked. "He's only one little critter. Right?"

Enthusiasm ran high as we piled into our family ranch wagon and embarked on our calf-fetching quest.

When we pulled into the dairy, several cows stood in a corral. The children spotted an adorable little black-and-white calf looking at us as though he knew he was destined to be our new farm addition. The kids were excited.

"Can we have that one, Daddy?" "He's so cute!" They exclaimed.

Unable to resist their excitement and batting eyelashes, we bought him and loaded him into the van.

"Let's lay down some cardboard and plastic to protect the interior carpet," I suggested, crafting a makeshift cow diaper—just in case.

Little did we know that this little feller was a master urine expeller. From the moment we hit the road, he began to turn our vehicle into a mobile fountain of bovine relief.

For the entire 30-minute ride, he had endless urine to share with us as he drooped his head over the seat and mooed in satisfaction. My wife sat in horror, and the kids laughed their heads off.

"He stinks, Daddy!" Becky exclaimed as she pinched her nose.

When we stopped, an intense aroma greeted us that rivaled the largest dairy farms in the world. The steady stream of bladder water had seeped through every nook and cranny of the cardboard and soaked our van's carpet.

"You would think that calf was competing in a urination marathon," I said as I shook my head.

Five years later, we could still smell the cattle ranch inside the vehicle on a hot day.

"This is our unique ranch-scented air freshener," my wife joked.

"Yes, it is farm-to-car freshness; a genuine organic experience," I replied.

As you can guess, we learned the hard way that hauling cows in a minivan was no bovine bliss.

After everyone voted, "It's unanimous," I declared. "We're investing in a proper trailer. Goodbye *moo-van*, hello *moo-ver* wagon."

The laughs and memories will forever linger, like that unmistakable scent in our family car.

[30]

Minivan to Moo-van (Digital Depiction)

Takeaways and Lessons Learned:

1. **Embrace the Unexpected**: The author's humorous experience of transporting a calf in a minivan highlights the importance of embracing unexpected moments in life. While things may not always go as planned, these experiences can create lasting memories and bring joy and laughter to our lives.
2. **Learn from Mistakes**: The misadventure of hauling a cow in a minivan teaches a valuable lesson about learning from mistakes. Sometimes, trying unconventional methods can lead to unforeseen consequences, but these moments offer opportunities to learn and make better decisions in the future.

---

[30] Tool, D. E. (2024). Calf In The Van [Digital depiction]. Online. https://chatgpt.com/c/a9d97728-b6ef-4edd-b1e2-02dbe9a44e01

3. **The Importance of Adaptability**: The story underscores the need for adaptability and resourcefulness. When faced with an unexpected challenge, the author and his family adapted quickly, creating a makeshift solution. This ability to adjust and find humor in the situation made the experience more manageable and memorable.

Reflection Questions for Application

1. **How Do I Embrace Unexpected Challenges in My Life?**
   - Reflect on a recent unexpected challenge you faced. How did you respond to it? Did you find ways to adapt and see the humor in the situation? Consider how you can better embrace unexpected moments and turn them into positive experiences.
2. **What Lessons Have I Learned from My Mistakes?**
   - Think about a time when you tried something unconventional that didn't go as planned. What lessons did you learn from that experience? How have those lessons influenced your decisions and actions since then?
3. **How Can I Cultivate Adaptability and Resourcefulness?**
   - Reflect on your ability to adapt to new and challenging situations. How can you cultivate a mindset of resourcefulness and adaptability in your daily life? Consider ways to develop these skills and apply them to future challenges, turning potential setbacks into opportunities for growth and learning.

17

Victor's Payback

Finding God's Provision in Financial Turmoil

Moments arise at times when faith, provision, and miraculous intervention intertwine in a remarkable display of the Lord's goodness.

In the previous chapters, I shared wondrous stories of God's direct response to our specific prayers. Now, let me take you to a season without unicorns and rainbows—when my Heavenly Father, in His unfathomable grace, provided for us in a way that left us awe-struck, grateful, and humbled.

Life seemed perfect until financial struggles threatened to overwhelm us. I had injured my back and was out of work for two months. We were so broke we joked that our picture might end up on food stamps. However, we never needed those because the Lord provided for us.

Though grocery stamps are ok, we trusted God to supply our needs rather than rely on the government. I trust the government about as much as I trust gas station sushi.

Ann, a devoted stay-at-home mother, watched as our financial ship entered turbulent waters. We pinched pennies so hard that we gave Lincoln a nosebleed. As we teetered on the brink, empty pantries loomed, and we wondered if our belly buttons would soon rub blisters on our backbones.

My wife and I confronted our predicament one early morning as the sunrise painted soft hues across the sky.

"Well, Ann, as I see it, three options lay before us like divergent paths in a dense forest:

1. Succumb to worry and let fear gnaw at our hope.

2. Seek solace by living on governmental cheese.

3. Make a leap of faith and trust our needs to God's faithfulness—a path we have walked countless times before." I said, with Godfidence.

A crucial lesson had already been etched in my soul—the Lord stands as the ultimate provider, while I am but a vessel through which His provisions flow. My job is a resource. He is THE Source. Simple truths like these often escape us, taken for granted in our daily routines.

When we recognize that the Creator of the universe is our source for all things, we experience extreme liberation, an assurance that emanates like a warm embrace. After all, the Almighty parted the waters, not Moses; He crumbled Jericho's walls, not Joshua; and He answered the widow's plea, not Elijah.

We could hide this need from our children or involve them in this critical family decision and let them see God work again. If I said I wasn't discouraged, I would be lying.

"Oh Lord, show me the way." I prayed.

All of a sudden, little Isaac bounded into the room, clutching his giant, treasured picture Bible in his tiny hands.

"More Bible, Daddy, More Bible!"

In that simple act, I found the answer I was seeking—get into the Word. Our eyes found refuge in the sacred verses that held timeless guidance. Permit me to share a few:

- **(Proverbs 3:5-6 NLT)** "Trust in the Lord with all your heart; do not depend on your own understanding. Seek his will in all you do, and he will show you which path to take."

- **(John 14:27 NLT)** "Peace I leave with you, my peace, I give you; not as the world gives do I give to you. Do not let your hearts be troubled or fearful."
- **(Philippians 4:19 NLT)** "This same God who takes care of me will supply all your needs from his glorious riches..."
- **(Philippians 4:6-7 NLT)** "Don't worry about anything; instead, pray about everything. Tell God what you need and thank him for all he has done..."
- **(Luke 11:11-13 NLT)** "You fathers—if your children ask for a fish, do you give them a snake instead? Or do you give them a scorpion if they ask for an egg? Of course not! So, if you sinful people know how to give good gifts to your children, how much more will your heavenly Father give the Holy Spirit to those who ask him."

Enriched by these verses, we chose to trust God's providence. Gathering around the piano bench, we knelt and prayed, simple yet sincere. It sounded like this:

"Heavenly Father, we know that you are already aware of our needs. It comforts us that You will provide food for our table and help us pay our bills. Thank You for being behind the scenes and controlling the scenes You are behind. We believe in You as a family and will not fear our circumstances. Into Your capable hands, we place our needs, Lord. In Jesus' name, amen." I petitioned with a thankful heart.

Then, each child prayed, except Becky, who was a baby.

"Dear Jesus, it's me, Isaac. We're running low on mac 'n' cheese and cereal, and Mom says we can't eat cookies for dinner. Please help us get more food, so that we don't have to eat Broccoli. Also, make Daddy's back better so he can work again. Amen."

Jacob folded his hands, squeezed his eyes shut, and added:

"Hi God, it's me, Jacob. Can you help Mommy and Daddy? Also, if You have time, can we have a puppy someday? Thank You! Amen!"

In God's eyes, I believe their simple, little prayers had more power than ours. After reading and discussing these verses, our spirits rekindled, and our faith fortified. The call for "more Bible" led us to a renewed trust.

The relief and comfort that followed our prayers were like a warm blanket on a cold night, reassuring us that we were not alone in our struggles.

Our trust in the Almighty was not in vain. A miracle happened when our breakfast was interrupted by a phone call.

A voice on the other end inquired, "Hello, is this Mark Bruton, the son of Gyneth and Richard?"

"Yes, this is Mark. May I ask who's calling?" I replied.

"Mark, this is Victor. You don't know me, but I knew your parents many years ago. I have something I need to confess."

He let out a deep sigh. "Decades ago, I borrowed $300 from your parents and never repaid it. Guilt has hounded me for thirty years, and I need to make it right."

A wave of surprise washed over me. "Victor, my parents are both deceased, and I assure you they would forgive you and tell you to forget about it if they were here. I admire your honesty and integrity. Those character traits are rare nowadays."

Victor's voice grew more determined. "No, I must repay this debt. I will send you the money in two-week installments."

I expressed heartfelt gratitude and sensed the weight of his sincerity.

"Partner, your timing is impeccable. We are a Christian family and have prayed for our needs to be met. Your call is an immediate answer to those prayers."

He sounded relieved. "I'm glad to hear that. I'll get your address and send the first payment soon."

Ann sat there with her mouth wide open when I got off the phone. The kids were ecstatic. They were so excited that the Lord had already answered our prayer; they believed it justified the need for ice cream to celebrate. We agreed, and we sensed the Lord smiled from above.

We anticipated our first payment of $150; half of the $300 owed. Within three days, a manila envelope arrived. Inside was a letter:

"Dear Mark, I wish I could apologize to your parents for taking so long to repay this money. Enclosed, you will find a check for $1,800. That is the first payment. The second one will come in two weeks. PS. Thirty years accrue much interest."

The envelope bore the alias Victor Payback. We never got his actual last name. There was no address, just the name. It was apparent he wanted to remain anonymous, or was it an Angel?

The other remittance of $1,800 came in two weeks. We remembered **Malachi 3:10:** "Bring all the tithes into the storehouse… I will open the windows of Heaven for you. I will pour out a blessing so great you won't have enough room to take it in! Try it! Put me to the test!"

Amidst our astonishment, we grasped the grandeur of God's providence—our humble prayer met with lavish abundance. The story of "Victor's payback" etched itself into our hearts as a testament to the boundless faithfulness of our Creator. It reinforced the phrase, 'The Lord will provide.'

This phrase is not mere rhetoric but a living, breathing reality. Faith, in its true essence, isn't just believing that God can act; it's knowing, with unshakable certainty that He will.

The smiles on our faces, our children's laughter, and this dear man's anonymous gift bore witness to the divine Father when we placed our hope in His provision. Praise be to God, the ultimate

Provider, who showers His love upon us, proving again that He is faithful beyond measure.

Think about this: As Jesus was faithful from earth to the Father in Heaven, so is He loyal to you on earth from Heaven. Hallelujah!

O you of little faith,
God has not failed you yet!
When all looks dark and gloomy,
You do so soon forget—

Forget that He has led you,
And gently cleared your way;
On clouds has poured His sunshine,
And turned your night to day.

And if He's helped you to this point,
He will not fail you now;
How it must wound His loving heart
To see your anxious brow!

Oh! doubt not any longer,
To Him, commit your way,
Whom in the past you trusted,
[31]And is "just the same today."

Author unknown

---

[31] Cowman, L. B. E., & Reimann, J. (1958, August 15). Poem: "Oh Thou Of Little Faith". Christianity.com. Retrieved June 29, 2023, from https://www.christianity.com/devotionals/streams-in-the-desert/

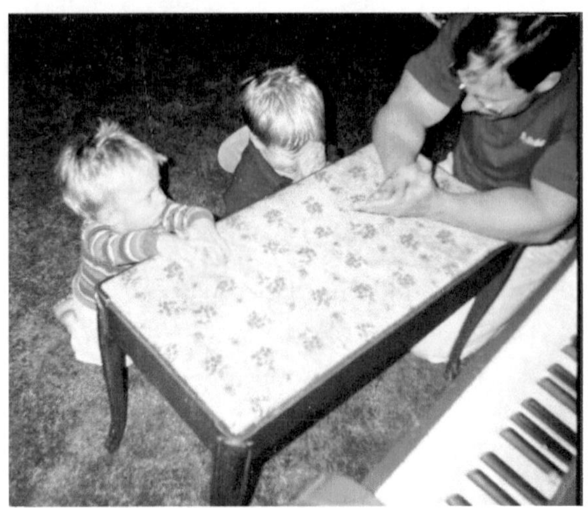

Praying with the boys 1994

[32]

Digital depiction

[32] Tool, D. E. (2023). Victor Payback [Digital depiction]. Online. https://chatgpt.com/c/6988419c-9a75-4319-bb82-6a2adfea6df5

Takeaways and Lessons Learned:

1. **Trusting God's Provision:** The story highlights the profound lesson of trusting God's provision, even during seemingly insurmountable challenges. Through the example of the author's experience, readers learn that placing their faith in God's unwavering care can lead to miraculous interventions that exceed their expectations. This takeaway underscores the importance of relying on God's faithfulness rather than succumbing to fear or worldly solutions.
2. **The Power of Simple Faith:** The narrative emphasizes the significance of childlike faith, as demonstrated by the author's children and their heartfelt prayers. By engaging with the Bible and embracing its promises, the family's simple yet sincere trust in God's Word catalyzes His miraculous response. This lesson encourages readers to approach their relationship with God with simplicity and a genuine belief in His promises.
3. **God's Timing and Generosity:** Through the unexpected act of an anonymous giver, the story illustrates the profound truth that God's provision often arrives in unexpected ways and at just the right moment. The generous gift addressed the family's immediate needs and surpassed their expectations. This takeaway teaches us to remain patient, open, and grateful, recognizing that God's timing and generosity are beyond human comprehension.

Reflection Questions for application:

1. In times of financial or personal struggles, how do you tend to respond – by relying on your own efforts, becoming anxious, or entrusting your situation to God? How can you

cultivate a deeper trust in God's provision based on the examples shared in the story?

2. Consider your approach to prayer and faith. Are there areas in your life where you could embrace a more childlike faith, like the author's children? How can you actively engage with the Word of God to strengthen your faith and encourage a deeper connection with Him?
3. Reflect on instances when you've experienced God's provision or unexpected blessings. How did these experiences impact your faith and perspective? How can you become more attuned to recognizing God's timing and generosity in your daily life, fostering a greater sense of gratitude and reliance on Him?

18

Trusting God's Direction at Life's Crossroads

Unveiling God's Five-Step Path to Clarity in Decision Making

In 1995, my dissatisfaction with employment in the dog-eat-dog corporate world became unbearable. As a journeyman meat cutter, I received great pay and excellent health benefits. Yet, an inner stirring—a "holy discontent"—suggested that my Heavenly Father had a different career in store. What could it be? With a family to support, quitting wasn't an option. Still, I sensed He was about to unveil new opportunities, filling me with anticipation and hope for what would come.

One Sunday evening, I returned to the rustic mountain church where my journey had begun years before—Brother Bill Bryan's congregation. This quaint little country assembly, a tight-knit community of farmers and ranchers, was a place that embraced old-fashioned values and played a pivotal role in my spiritual growth. The smell of worn wooden pews and the faint scent of mountain pine brought back fond memories.

Two towering cowboys, each about 6'5", dressed in authentic Western attire, caught my attention. They were as masculine as John Wayne, and the grip in their handshake tightened my shoelaces. Their broad shoulders seemed capable of using a super-wide janitor broom for a coat hanger.

These fellas were tough enough to gargle peanut butter, floss with a railroad tie, and comb their hair with a four-bottom plow. Yet, they exuded the grace of gentlemen. They wore large-brimmed cowboy hats that shadowed their sun-worn faces. Their Wrangler jeans were pressed and creased, and their western shirts starched. They also wore large gold belt buckles and polished boots.

These young, sturdy brothers were prosperous ranchers alongside their father on the prestigious Baird Ranch. We bonded right away, and their hearty laughter echoed through the small church as they enjoyed my humor. Their hearts matched the size of their frames, radiating warmth and acceptance. Our family visited the mountain church every Sunday evening, which deepened my connection with the two lads and made us feel welcome and included in their community.

Months passed, and the Baird boys approached me one Sunday for a serious conversation.

“Hey, Pard,” said the older of the two, Brock, tipping his hat. "Got a proposition for ya.”

Curious, I followed them into a small room. “What’s on your mind, fellers?”

John, the other brother, jumped in. “There is an open position on our ranch for a head foreman. It includes a charming and spacious farmhouse, a decent salary, and plenty of room for your kids to roam. We want you to consider the position.”

My instinct urged me to say yes without delay. Still, I had learned the value of waiting on the divine plan and prayerful consideration. Ann and I were thrilled by the prospect of raising our children on a vast mountain homestead.

“Brock, John,” I replied. “This sounds like a lifetime opportunity, but we must pray and seek the Lord before making such a big life choice.”

They nodded. “That's understood, Pard, and we respect that. Take your time. The job will be here when and if you’re ready.”

Their patience and respect for my priority were testaments to their character.

This life-altering choice was not a minor one. It would be foolish to leave my secure job unless I knew my Heavenly Father was the orchestrator of it. But how does one know if it is God who is leading you?

When faced with complex decisions, I have always relied on a five-step process. These principles, not from any book or sermon, were revealed to me by the Holy Spirit, based on the Bible's teachings. They have never failed me and have always helped me decipher difficult choices.

Before I share the miraculous answer the Lord gave us concerning this move to the Baird ranch, let me share these principles because they will also help you make the right decisions and safeguard your future. Again, these are not my principles; they are straight from Heaven, and you can trust them to lead you right.

When you navigate a complex situation, ask yourself five Biblical inquiries while seeking direction from the Father in Heaven. Your questions must pass through all five gates. Here is the key: if you can't answer "yes" to all five questions, then the answer is "no," or wait. If you can affirm yes to each one, then the answer is yes. Remember the prudence of **(Proverbs 3:5-6 NLT)**.

The Five Principles for Decision-Making:

1. **Is the door open or closed?**
   Firstly, ask if the door is open when facing a crucial decision. If it's closed, ask God to open it if it's His will. If He doesn't open it, then it's not His will. Just because a door is open doesn't mean you must go through it.

Paul's example in **2 Corinthians 2:12-13 (NLT)** shows that even though **God opened** a door, he did not go through it because he lacked peace.

2. **Do I have the peace of God about the situation?**
(**Colossians 3:15, NIV)** "Let the peace of Christ rule in your hearts since you were called to peace as members of one body. And be thankful." If you don't have peace, stop! Wait for peace from God. *He always leads with His peace.*
3. **What advice do your wise counselors give?**
(Proverbs 11:14, MEV) "Where there is no counsel, the people fall, but there is safety in the multitude of counselors." Seek advice from godly advisors—men and women who will assist you in looking at all angles of a scenario. This approach in my life has been invaluable.
4. **Have I obeyed the last thing the Lord told me to do?**
Evaluate your obedience to God's previous instructions. If you have ignored the previous one, God will not lead you to the next step. For example, if you need to make things right with someone, do it before moving forward.
5. **What is the Word of God revealing to me?**
(Psalm 119:105, NLT) "Your word is a lamp to guide my feet and a light for my path." Seek His mind through meditation in His word. The Bible provides timeless principles, moral values, and insights into God's character and desires. It reflects our hearts' intentions and humility.

Someone once asked Brother Bill how he remained so loyal to the Lord for over sixty years. "Stay in the Word!" he replied.

Applying the 5 Principles to My Decision About the Baird Ranch

Returning to the Baird ranch story, I subjected the decision to the five questions mentioned above.

1. **Was the door open?** Yes, they offered me the foreman position.
2. **Did I have the peace of God?** Yes, the previous answers provided assurance.
3. **What advice did wise counsellors give?** We consulted church leaders, which prompted thoughtful discussion and considerations. After we considered the pros and cons, they believed the move could be beneficial.
4. **Had I obeyed the last thing He told me to do?** Yes, I had no unresolved issues and no grudges. The Lord did convict me to ask the boss for forgiveness for growing bitter with his underhanded shenanigans with his staff. I did this and, therefore, obeyed.
5. **What is the Word of God revealing to me?** I needed specific guidance for this life-altering choice. Ann and I agreed that I would submit my resignation the next day. But something was missing.

After reviewing my checklist, I found that everything was aligned—the door open, supportive counsel, resolved obedience, and inner peace. However, a direct message from the Bible was missing. When I went to bed that night, I asked the Lord to give me clear direction from His word before I terminated my employment.

When the sun came up and greeted me with a new, fresh day, I went to prayer and opened my Bible. I sought a specific verse and yearned for direct communication, saying, "Father, I must hear from You before I submit this letter and surrender my position today."

I picked up my favorite daily devotional, "Streams in the Desert," dated March 17. The first words revealed on the page: ***"Stay there till***

I bring word." "I'll stay where You've put me; I will, dear Lord, 5 ough I wanted so badly to go..."[33]

A sense of clarity washed over me; this was my Heavenly Father's answer. There were tears when I shared this revelation with Ann, but we praised the Lord for His direction. "Sweetheart, He has never led us wrong," I said, with Godfidence.

Six months later, we learned that the Baird Ranch had gone bankrupt. God's wisdom and faithfulness protected our family. His role as a gentle shepherd led us down the right path, which was cause for celebration, not discouragement.

However, the Lord did have a better career alternative for me, and He worked miracles to make it happen. The exciting details of this story will greet you in the next chapter.

[34]

Digital depiction of the Baird brothers

---

[33] Cowman, L. (2024, August 1). August First. Streams in the Desert. Retrieved August 1, 2024, from Cowman, L. B. E.; Reimann, Jim. Zondervan. Kindle Edition.

[34] Tool, D. E. (2024). The Baird Brothers [Digital depiction]. Online. https://chatgpt.com/c/9a047a65-b009-4492-bb90-d8e49dd59e32

Takeaways and Lessons Learned:

1. **Divine Clarity through God's Five-Step Path:** In moments of life-altering decision-making, following the five-step process rooted in biblical principles can provide clarity and assurance. The steps include seeking open doors, discerning God's peace, seeking wise counsel, obeying God's previous instructions, and aligning decisions with God's revealed Word. Trusting and diligently applying these steps can guide individuals toward God's intended path.
2. **God's Perfect Timing and Wisdom:** The story underscores the importance of waiting for God's perfect timing and seeking His wisdom before making significant life choices. Although external factors may seem favorable, it is crucial to prioritize seeking God's specific guidance and peace before proceeding. Obedience to His leading, even if it goes against personal desires, ultimately aligns individuals with His sovereign plan.
3. **The Transformative Power of Scripture:** The Word of God is a powerful tool for decision-making. Meditating on Scripture provides divine guidance, self-reflection, and humility before God. By seeking direct messages from God's Word and allowing them to shape decisions, individuals can experience a deeper connection with God's will and a clearer understanding of their paths.

Reflection Questions for Application:

1. How can I apply the five-step process outlined in the story to my current decision-making processes? Have I prioritized God's leading by watching for open doors, discerning God's peace, seeking wise counsel, obeying previous instructions, and aligning decisions with God's Word?

2. What areas of my life might I need to exercise more patience and wait for God's perfect timing and wisdom, even when circumstances appear favorable? How can I cultivate a mindset of trust in God's sovereign plan?
3. How has the transformative power of Scripture played a role in my past decision-making? Am I actively seeking God's guidance daily through His Word in my current decision-making processes? How can I deepen my reliance on God's Word for clarity and direction?

19

A Fulfilling Career Unveiled: The Journey of an Educator

PRAISE: The Key That Unlocks Dreams

The Lord shielded and guided us from making a move that would have been disastrous for our family. Despite this, I still longed to leave the grocery industry. I sensed that God had something better for me than working in a 34-degree cooler, daily, akin to working in a penguin breeding sanctuary.

As one of the pastors at our church, I felt valuable and content in my spiritual life. Yet, something was missing in my vocation. One night, overwhelmed with discouragement after the potential opportunity with the Bairds didn't materialize, I pondered my future and expressed my discontentment to my wife.

Feeling trapped, I sensed the need to seek the Lord alone, praying for clarity. In the stillness, a life-changing principle from Scripture came to mind—praise.

A conversation began with the still, small voice inside, as it whispered to my heart, "Mark, who do you remember in the Bible who was trapped in prison but didn't deserve it?"

"Paul and Silas," I replied.

"That's right, and what did they do to get out of that undeserved predicament? Did they complain and grumble or use their fighting skills?"

"No, they sang songs of praise, and the bars fell. Despite having every right to complain, Paul and Silas praised their way out instead!"

The gentle instruction from the Holy Spirit settled into my thick head: "Quit complaining and start praising God. Don't whine, shine!"

I also remembered the battles of the Old Testament, where God commanded the armies to put the tribe of Judah on the frontline. Judah means praise. If a mighty army came against me, I would prefer the Navy Seals, Marine raiders, Army Rangers, and the Green Berets in front, not the marching band!

Try to envision the scene; can't you see them? Expressions adorned their faces like bug-eyed Don Knotts as they stared at each other in fear, bewilderment, and so nervous that they shook like a fifty-cent ladder. So, they cried out,

"Lord, there are so many of them! Do we hear you right? Shouldn't we have our strongest and best warriors in the front of the battle?"

"No, put the choir in front and rely on Me!"

Many wonder why He would do this. The Divine general taught them that their strength lay not in their weapons and skills, but in the almighty God. They had to acknowledge that He was the victor by praising Him in the battle.

"'Not by might, nor by power, but by my Spirit,' says the Lord Almighty." **(Zechariah 4:6, NIV)**

Like all of us, they needed to know that Jehovah defended them and was mightier than any enemy. This praise principle demonstrated to those coming against them that they were fighting the creator of the universe, not puny humans.

"That's it!" I thought to myself. "This is the truth I needed."

The message is clear: If you want out of a lousy job, praise. Suppose you are in a health crisis, praise. That night, I prayed for forgiveness for my complaints. I was grateful for my employment and didn't want to show discontentment with what God gave me.

The usual bedtime custom was to tell a fun and suspenseful story to my kids and then kneel beside the bed and pray with them. That night, I prayed,

"Father, I hurt!"

"I know," came the assurance.

"The weight is too heavy; please help me!"

A scripture verse echoed in my mind. "Sorrow may last for the night, but joy comes in the morning." (Psalm 30:5)

Deep in my soul, I sensed that the creator of Heaven and Earth was about to bring a significant change into my life that would redefine my career and purpose. Sorrow still clung to me that night. Yet, I felt a deep peace, as if my Heavenly Father said, "I've got you, son, and everything will be all right; just start praising me for what I am about to do." This reassurance brought a wave of relief, a beacon of hope in uncertainty.

As the morning dawned, I noticed that the television was on. "That's strange," I thought. "We never watch TV in the mornings."

Abruptly, an African-American speaker appeared on the screen. This man wasn't your usual money-grabbing, hair-spray evangelist, but a persuasive orator I had never seen before. His words pierced my heart and resonated as if tailored for me.

He stared into my eyes and asked, "What hinders your dream? Yes, you, I am talking to you!" His forceful glare somehow comforted me.

"What's the matter? What holds you back from accomplishing your dreams: an exam? Get out of that bed, stand up, square your shoulders back, and prepare for that test! Go and get the life you want!"

His message was so direct that if I changed stations, I was sure I would find him on every channel. How did he know I put my career on hold because of a test I couldn't pass?

My academic and pedagogical training prepared me to be an educator. However, this aspiration remained dormant for 12 years due to my ongoing battle with a state math exam and its daunting time limit.

I passed all the other required teacher exams with ease, but discouragement still hung over me like a dark cloud because math had always been like a coiled rattlesnake waiting to strike me with its venom.

The numbers never gave me a problem, but then the devil came along and threw the alphabet into the mix, and that's where the handle fell out of the shovel.

The man continued, and clarity and certainty began to surge within me. Embracing the call to be an educator became my new goal—a vocation that would impact people's lives more than my job in the grocery industry. This revelation was transformative, filling me with inspiration and hope for the future.

One of my favorite quotes comes from Little Lord Fauntleroy's mother: "The world should be a better place because a man or woman has lived."

After sharing this revelation with my wife, we rejoiced and realized that 'joy indeed came in the morning.' Still, the rigorous path ahead loomed. But with a newfound determination and courage, we faced the challenges ahead, knowing that we were on the right path.

Returning to postgraduate school was a significant commitment, requiring a year and a half of additional courses due to the twelve-year gap since graduation. On top of that, the Colorado Place exams were on the horizon—four four-hour-long tests, each costing $100.

A profound sense of faith and reliance enveloped me. I surrendered to my heavenly King, acknowledged His call, trusted His wisdom, and sought His provision, encouraged by the quote, "If He brings you to it, He will get you through it."

This test was my Red Sea. I only needed to step into it with Godfidence and watch the path open before me.

"The Lord will provide money for school," I said to Ann with a confident smile.

I didn't know how He would do it, but I trusted He would provide for us, even though fewer hours at work would create a challenge.

Determined to keep Ann as a stay-at-home mom, we agreed to reduce my work schedule to 28-32 hours per week. The extra time would allow me to attend classes and maintain a semblance of income. With God's help, our financial obligations were met, and my studies progressed. Out of necessity, I secured the assistance of three tutors for algebra, geometry, and trigonometry, and my scores began to soar.

The Lord surprised us again with an unexpected financial gift. Having injured my back about a year earlier, I went through months of extensive physical therapy and meetings with surgeons. We thought that was the end after they released me back to work.

However, not long after I returned to work, Ann opened the mail one day and, with eyes the size of silver dollars, found a settlement check for $20,000. This money caught us off guard because we had no idea it was coming. We were in shock. The amount was perfect to cover my reduced hours at work, pay off my school debt, and settle the farm loan.

Miracles like these prompted me to write this book with a thankful heart, to capture and share the memories of God's goodness in my life. Friend, you can trust the man who died for you!

The New Path: From City Market to the Classroom

During my internship, the Lord directed me to the perfect elementary and secondary mentors aligned with my aspiration to teach health and physical education.

After completing my internship and using the five questions for decision-making mentioned in the previous chapter, I was confident that it was God's will for me to resign from City Market. I began a period of substitute teaching and embraced every subject and grade level. The pay was insufficient to support a family. Still, we held on to our faith and believed it to be a temporary stepping stone.

After receiving my Colorado teaching license, I taught summer school to learners who needed to catch up during the regular year. One afternoon, while on my lunch hour, a phone call from an administrator altered my life course.

"Mr. Bruton," came the voice on the line. "Your name has come up often as a potential teacher who would be an asset to our district. There is a need to fill a full-time elementary Health and Physical Education position. Can you come for an interview tomorrow at 3:00 pm?"

"Absolutely, and thank you for the opportunity!" I replied.

The position offered was at the school where I was a student teacher, available due to my mentors' transfer to the new middle school. Once again, God showed His kindness through this new open door and gave me favor with teachers and administrators in the district. After I met with the team, the Principal handed me the keys and said, "Welcome aboard; everyone is thrilled to have you on our staff."

"Thank you, sir; I won't let the team down."

After I received the keys, I went straight to the gymnasium. As I stepped into the room for the first time, the scent of polished wood and the faint echoes of past and future games made me smile. Sunlight streamed through the high windows, casting a glow on the floor.

Children's laughter seemed to bounce off the walls, creating a symphony hinting at the space's joy and energy. The vibrant colors of the equipment—red, blue, green, and yellow—contrasted against the neutral walls. The soft, rubbery texture of the mats underfoot reminded me of the countless activities that awaited. My heart swelled with excitement and anticipation, knowing this gym would become a place of growth and discovery for my students and me.

Overwhelmed with the gravity of this fulfilled dream, I knelt in the middle of the gym and praised the God who made it all happen. This contract began my incredible 31-year adventure as an educator, and I have loved every second of it. Retirement is an option now, but I feel strong and energetic and, by God's grace, have no desire to quit. The Good Shepherd will let me know when to cross that river.

The satisfaction and contentment I have derived from my career are immeasurable. No one could be happier than I am. It has been my privilege to teach diverse subjects and grade levels. One of my favorites was being a professor in the Exercise Sports Science department at Western Colorado University for a decade.

The Lord's goodness shines through as He paved the way, equipped me, and transformed my dream into a lifelong journey of fulfillment and purpose.

It is a beautiful reward to lead students and athletes to Christ. With their parents' permission, I have also conducted Bible studies with them in my home. Without a doubt, being a teacher is my true calling and ministry.

The journey began with a twenty-five-year span in the United States; my story took an unexpected turn as God led me to Norway for the past six years. Now, I find myself in an international school surrounded by students and teachers from diverse corners of the world. The story of that adventure lies ahead.

[35]

Digital Depiction

Takeaways and Lessons Learned:

1. **Embrace Divine Guidance and Timing:** The story underscores the importance of trusting God's timing and guidance. While we may have desires and dreams, we must remain patient, listen for His voice, and stay faithful to His path. The author's journey highlights that God's plans often unfold unexpectedly, and His protection and provision become evident when we follow His lead.
2. **The Power of Praise and Perspective:** The story emphasizes the transformative power of praise and a positive perspective in the face of challenges and uncertainty. The author's realization that praise can break down the bars of perceived limitations is a powerful reminder that our attitudes and reactions can impact our circumstances. If we choose gratitude and praise rather than complaint and negativity, our

[35] Tool, D. E. (2023). *Return to teaching* [Digital depiction]. Online. https://chatgpt.com/c/dd8ca2ba-5dd1-4cfa-aa20-1c7b987fe4bb

outlook can be shifted and doors to new opportunities can be open.

3. **Faith and Perseverance through Challenges:** The narrative showcases the importance of unwavering faith and perseverance in the pursuit of one's calling. Despite obstacles such as academic struggles, financial constraints, and career transitions, the author's commitment to his teaching vocation remained steadfast. The story underscores that challenges and setbacks are opportunities for growth and reliance on God's strength to overcome.

Reflection Questions for Application:

- **Am I Open to Divine Guidance?** Reflect on when you felt a strong desire for change or something better. Did you seek guidance from your Heavenly Father, intuition, or a sense of purpose? How might embracing patience and trusting a divine plan have influenced your choices and outcomes?
- **How Can I Shift My Perspective?** Think about a current challenge or area of discontentment in your life. How might adopting an attitude of praise and gratitude influence your perspective? What steps can you take to replace complaint and negativity with a focus on the positive aspects of your situation, and how might this change your outlook?
- **What Dreams Have I Put on Hold?** Consider aspirations or dreams you may have set aside due to obstacles or self-doubt. How have these dreams continued to resonate within you? Reflect on the story's message about facing challenges head-on and persevere in the pursuit of your calling. What steps can you take to overcome obstacles and reignite your passion for those dreams?

PART 3

Navigating The Depths of Failure:

"The Best Of Men Are but Men At Best"
--- Unknown---

20

The Scars That Have Shaped Me

How God Meets Us In Failure: A Transparent Account of Imperfection

The previous chapters have brimmed with hope, faith, praise, and miraculous answers to prayer, painting a picture of optimism and divine intervention.

However, this chapter reveals a thread of darkness I cannot omit. I unveil this portion of my life story with remorse and a heart heavy, but also full of optimism.

It has been said, **"The best of men are but men at best."** I relate to this phrase all too well.

As I share this chapter of my life's story, please know that it is painful, and I am aware that it might tarnish the image I have sought to cultivate as a Christian author. Nevertheless, my purpose is not to portray an idealized version of myself. This book is about God's goodness, not mine.

For my fellow misfits, the not-so-perfect people, the broken halo club—those who have blown it, but still find the Lord faithful and loving despite their failures—I write this story with openness and transparency for you.

Have you disappointed your Heavenly Father, spouse, family, or yourself? May this dark season of my life encourage you. Remember, we all have a sinful nature that fights for control, every day. Paul described this in **Galatians 5:17 (NLT):**

"The sinful nature wants to do evil, which is the opposite of what the Spirit wants. And the Spirit gives us desires that are the opposite of what the sinful nature desires. These two forces are in a constant fight with each other, so you are not free to carry out your good intentions."

"Two forces surge within my breast;
One is foul, and the other is blessed.
The new I love, the old I hate.
The one I feed will dominate." [36]

— Anonymous

The story I now recount is one of a love that faltered and a marriage that crumbled. Though united by devotion, Ann and I found ourselves on an unforeseen path.

When a marriage falls apart, two people share the blame, not just one. Many people focus on their spouse's imperfections to justify their own faults, contributing to the relationship's collapse; I will not do that here.

The glow that adorned our bond dimmed due to neglect, and I take responsibility for it. The flames that warmed our hearts grew cold, and a sinister force seized its moment in the chill.

Like others, we allowed indifference and apathy to infiltrate the sacred space of our fifteen-year partnership. Satan took advantage, casting his shadow over our haven. In a moment of weakness, the enemy of our souls took hold.

---

[36] Anonymous, A. (n.d.). Two Natures at War. Goodreads. Retrieved June 15, 2023, from https://www.goodreads.com/quotes/507804-two-natures-beat-within-my-breast-the-one-is-foul?fbclid=IwY2xjawEa3JlleHRuA2FlbQIxMAABHXNs6yHY_sHVNi_6tqhSdy-tbY3CVVn51585qOaiVrLoD4TLm5ggQDWp8A_aem_uKoZjuSTzCAjtHZM8hyfkQ

"I can't believe this is happening," Ann said, her voice breaking.

"I know," I replied, feeling the weight of our crumbling marriage. "I let my guard down, and now we're here."

"I don't know if we can fix this," she whispered, tears streaming down her face.

The fences, guardrails, and boundaries we built to protect our love had crumbled. In this dark vortex, I crossed a line I never believed I would. The embers of our relationship smoldered, and in complacency, I let the fire go out.

By agreement, we separated for one month. I returned to my family with a relentless determination to be the godly man I was called to be, but Ann's heart had become cold and hardened. Satan had lured me into an *emotional* affair with a student teacher under my mentorship.

"I can't believe I let this happen," I admitted, my voice heavy with regret and my heart burdened with the weight of my actions.

"Ann, I felt unloved and unappreciated at home," I confessed, my eyes downcast. "But I never meant to let it go this far."

The silence of our home was suffocating. The once warm and inviting spaces were now cold and shadowed, where every whisper of the wind through the cracks felt like the murmur of our faded love. The darkness seemed thicker each night as it pressed on me with the weight of a thousand elephants. Once vibrant and full of laughter, conversations with my wife were now distant and stilted, like trying to shout across an ever-widening abyss.

Ann perceived my emotional infidelity as much of a betrayal as a full-blown physical affair. Although I disagreed then, I now understand the truth from her perspective—a perspective I was blind to in the heat of the moment.

The emotional affair began as a gentle swirl of connection with the student teacher under my mentorship, but soon became a fierce vortex in which I was sucked in by her flattery, praise, admiration, and the simultaneous feeling of rejection at home. The remnants of my marriage disintegrated into the black hole of my choices.

This forbidden relationship followed Satan's usual deceptive pattern:

1. He knows **your bait.**
2. You end up being **hooked and reeled in**.
3. You find yourself **in the devil's frying pan** because of bad decisions.

I had taken the bait and was in the stage of being lured in when I tried with all my might to turn my heart towards home. During the month-long separation, I prayed, cried, and fasted. My sorrow mirrored David's in Psalms 50.

Though I hadn't betrayed my marital vows in a tangible or sexual sense, thoughts of the forbidden fruit invaded my mind with an insidious whisper. This attraction pulled me into a seductive current and a mental battleground. Determined not to break my marital vows, I fought like a First Knight guarding a king, but the ground beneath me crumbled. It was a futile battle, like trying to hold back a tsunami with a broom or trying to put out the fires of hell with a water pistol. The whirlpool of deceit consumed the last remnants of our marriage and left me adrift in its wake.

The struggle I experienced is echoed in the song: ***"Sin Will Take You Farther,"*** written by Mark Trammell:

As a child, I foolishly turned God away
Not knowing the heartache a sinner must face.
But God, in His goodness, has let me return
To share with His children this lesson I've learned.
Sin will take you farther than you want to go,
Slowly but wholly taking control.
Sin will leave you longer than you want to stay.

Sin will cost you far more than you want to pay.
So, with pleasure and promises, sin took control,
Leaving me dying with nothing to show.
Gone were my loved ones and my dearest friends;
Only a Savior could love me again.
Sin will take you farther than you want to go,
Slowly but wholly taking control.
Sin will leave you longer than you want to stay.
Sin will cost you far more than you want to pay. [37]

The tragedy extended its grip on my relationship with my Heavenly Father, leaving me shattered and feeling like a failure on multiple fronts. I was in a spiritual and emotional freefall, wearing a concrete parachute.

Amid the depths of my consequential sorrow, God's love shone through. In desperation, I prayed and cried out for a revelation of His mercy and forgiveness. A sign that would say, "I'm here; I still care about you, and I'm not done with you."

That sign came when I turned on the radio to distract myself. At that moment, as if orchestrated by divine hands, a country tune played on the airwaves. The lyrics of George Strait's famous song, **"Love Without End, Amen,"** resonated with my soul—a message of a father's unending love.

Love Without End, Amen
I got sent home from school one day
With a shiner on my eye.
Fightin' was against the rules, and it didn't matter why.

---

[37] Trammell, M. (2010, January 5). Sin Will Take You Farther. Flashlyrics. Retrieved June 19, 2024, from https://www.flashlyrics.com/lyrics/the-cathedrals/sin-will-take-you-farther-39

When Dad got home, I told that story just like I'd rehearsed.
Then, stood there on those tremblin' knees
And waited for the worst.
He said, "Let me tell you a secret about a father's love;
A secret that my daddy said was just between us."
He said, "Daddies don't just love their children
Every now and then. It's a love without end, amen!
It's a love without end, amen!
When I became a father in the spring of '81,
There was no doubt that stubborn boy
It was just like my father's son.
And when I thought my patience
had been tested to the end,
I took my daddy's secret and passed it on to him.
I said, "Let me tell you a secret about a father's love;
A secret that my daddy said was just between us."
I said, "Daddies don't just love their children
Every now and then. It's a love without end, amen!
It's a love without end, amen!"
Last night, I dreamed I died and stood outside those pearly gates.
When suddenly, I realized there must be some mistake
If they know half the things I've done.
They'll never let me in.
Then, somewhere from the other side, I heard those words again.
They said, "Let me tell you a secret about a father's love;
A secret that my daddy said was just between us.
You see, daddies don't just love their children
Every now and then. It's a love without end, amen!
It's a love without end, amen!" [38]

---

[38] Love Without End Amen - Aaron Barker / George Straight (n.d.). Love Without End, Amen. Letras. Retrieved June 21, 2023, from https://www.letras.mus.br/george-strait/38696/#google_vignette

With perfect timing, that song embraced me, offering solace and direction. It reminded me that, despite my shortcomings, God's love is without end. It extends beyond our faults and darkest moments. God's heart breaks when we go off course, but He does not cast us away. His grace transcends our mistakes, and His forgiveness knows no limits. Jesus died for sinners, not perfect people.

Please make no mistake: Even though we are forgiven, we must face the consequences of our sinful actions. But we remain the Heavenly Father's precious and loved children. He does not cast us away because of our countless faults.

For example, if my children go out and commit the most heinous crimes, it will not change the fact that they are my children. I will still love them even if it breaks my heart and disappoints me. How much deeper is God's love than ours?

The Bible says in **Romans 5:8 (NIV)**, *"God demonstrates his love for us in this: While we were **yet** sinners, Christ died for us."*

This truth bears repeating:

- *The Father's love surpasses our failures.*
- *His forgiveness knows no limits.*
- *Shattered lives become whole again in His hands.*

Consider the many Bible characters whose lives were riddled with colossal failure. Yet, those were the ones whom the Lord used in powerful ways.

Amidst our blunders, His grace carries us forward. Let not the weight of guilt and shame hold you captive; for each morning brings a fresh start and a clean slate.

The words of **Lamentations 3:23 (NLT)** remind us that God's mercy is renewed every day: *"Great is his faithfulness; his mercies begin afresh each morning."*

My trip from the precipice of despair was not swift or without its scars. Through repentance and God's everlasting mercy, I returned to the Lord's embrace. I realized that I was not beyond repair, even in my shattered state. God's love stitched the broken pieces of my life back together, and though the scars remain, they bear witness to His transformative power.

As I pour these words onto the page, tears of sorrow and gratitude blur my vision. The story of the end of my marriage to Ann is one of pain and regret, but it is also a tapestry woven with threads of faith, mercy, and renewal. I acknowledged and confessed my mistakes, faced the consequences of my actions, and found restoration in God's boundless love.

One final note: For years, I have seen many self-righteous Christians who look down their holy noses and stand in judgment of others who have fallen and failed, treating them as though they were damaged goods and, therefore, have no value after they blew it.

I have also witnessed pompous religious people who throw rocks at the wayward brother or sister and are often the ones who fall and fail. Remember, "it ain't no fun when the rabbit gets the gun!" The Bible clearly defines how we are to treat those who have wandered away and are trapped like a lamb caught in a mud pit. We are to ***restore*** one another, ***not stone*** one another.

(Galatians 6:1 NIV):
"Dear brothers and sisters, if another believer is overcome by some sin, you who are godly should gently and humbly help that person back onto the right path. And be careful not to fall into the same temptation yourself."

So, as this painful chapter finds its place within my legacy book, I write with a heart that has been both broken and healed. I share my story, not as a tale of despair, but as a testament to the enduring love of our Father, above.

He waits with open arms for all who stumble and offers redemption and renewal to those who seek it.

It is my prayer that this chapter's honesty and transparency will serve as a guide to safeguard you from making the same mistakes. Let us travel onward and upward, imperfect yet loved, knowing that the Father's love, without end, guides us through every trial and triumph.

[39]

Slow fade (Digital Depictions)

[39] Sad Couple growing apart - Tool, E. E. (2024). Sad couple growing apart [Digital depiction]. Online. https://chatgpt.com/c/69ff991c-b68f-4c48-945d-bd424097bb6b

 [40]

Seeking forgiveness and repentance

Takeaways and Lessons Learned:

- **The Fragility of Relationships:** The story underscores the delicate nature of relationships, especially within marriage. Neglect and indifference can erode even the strongest bonds, and it's essential to tend to the flame of love with intention and care. Keep throwing the wood of romance and value on the fire of your marriage.
- **The Destructive Power of Temptation:** The story illustrates how even the strongest and most steadfast individuals can be

[40] Mark seeks forgiveness and purpose - Tool, E. E. (2024). Mark seeks forgiveness and purpose [Digital depiction]. Online. https://chatgpt.com/c/69ff991c-b68f-4c48-945d-bd424097bb6b

lured into temptation. It reminds us that no one is immune to the enemy's strategies and that vigilance in guarding one's heart and mind is crucial. It also reminds us to pray for pastors. They are on the frontline of hell, and Satan wants to destroy them.

- **God's Unfailing Love and Redemption:** Through the authors' journey, we witness the unyielding nature of God's love and the power of redemption. Even in the face of failure and brokenness, God's grace can restore and heal, offering a fresh start and a path toward renewal. ***Remember, you do not have to make yourself clean to come to God; you come to God to be made clean in Christ.***

Reflection Questions for Application:

1. Am I tending to the relationships that matter most in my life, or am I inadvertently neglecting them in the busyness of life? How can I actively invest in nurturing and strengthening those connections? In what ways can I throw wood on the embers to keep the home fires burning?
2. What temptations or vulnerabilities have I encountered that could threaten my spiritual or personal well-being? How can I fortify myself against such temptations and seek accountability?
3. Do I genuinely believe in God's limitless grace and forgiveness in times of guilt and remorse over past mistakes? How can I embrace God's promise of a fresh start each day and move forward with a heart unburdened by past failures?

21

Embracing Change

A Fresh Start in an Unfamiliar Land: Relocating to Kansas

The year 2000 dawned like a fresh sunrise, signaling a new chapter in my life. The turmoil of the divorce had cast a shadow over my soul—a period of darkness I struggled to endure. Yet, amidst my distress, a new era unfolded. Our Heavenly Father works in mysterious ways; when one door closes, another opens. The year 2000, in particular, was significant as it marked the beginning of my journey towards healing and faith.

After some time, Cindy, my former intern, reemerged in my life. Our paths, once strictly professional, converged as we recognized shared interests and aspirations. Deciding to explore our relationship further, we embarked on a journey together.

However, Ann's presence lingered as legalities loomed. She wanted to remarry, but her new love lived in Kansas. Fear and dread gripped my heart as she sought to relocate our children eight hundred miles away, creating a legal nightmare. She had retained a ruthless attorney who pulled out all the stops to force me to surrender my kids to relocation. Even she was surprised by his antics. But it was too late. He had already set the ball in motion, and the thought of losing my children sent me spiraling into a deep darkness—a whirlwind of sadness that left me breathless.

I turned to prayer in these tumultuous waters, seeking solace and understanding from my Heavenly Father. I uttered words of praise and confusion through tear-filled eyes and a trembling heart. Why must my kids be taken from me? The reality of my children's impending relocation hung over my head like a dark hurricane forming, and I grappled with the wrenching heartache of separation.

Clinging to their clothes, I lay on my bed, tears of soul sorrow streaming down my face. In my anguish, I continued to seek the dear Lord for help—for a glimmer of light in my darkest hour. After I prayed, I sobbed for ten more minutes.

All at once, my prayer was answered in a miraculous way. The phone rang, and though I hesitated, something compelled me to answer.

"Answer that call, Mark."

A familiar voice, a long-lost acquaintance from my deceased sister's past, spoke on the other end. Tracy, my sister's best friend, was reaching out to me with an inexplicable urgency in her tone.

Memories of happier times resurfaced, and for a brief period, we talked about Sis. Then Tracy shared her reason for calling. She described an encounter she had thirty minutes before contacting me.

"Mark, I don't know what is happening in your life, but it must be complicated and painful. What I'm about to tell you scared me, yet comforted me at the same time, and I assure you it wasn't a dream or a hallucination. While driving today, I glanced over to the passenger seat, and your sister, Vandi, was there, smiling vibrantly. Her face changed to an expression of deep concern. Vandi told me, 'Tracy, you must call my brother, Mark, and tell him that everything will be all right!'"

As Tracy delivered the message from my sister from beyond, we cried. Her words, conveying my sister's encouragement, penetrated my broken spirit. The weight that burdened me started to lift, as hope and peace replaced misery. It was a moment of profound relief and comfort—a reassurance that Jesus cared about my broken heart and would somehow turn this around.

As the sun rose the following day, I followed my usual morning routine and sought guidance by meditating on the Bible. I found solace and direction in the story of Abraham's journey to an unfamiliar land. His Godfidence in the face of uncertainty resonated, inspiring me to embrace change, trust the divine plan, and begin a new chapter.

This was the verse the Lord gave me that morning: **(Hebrews 11:8 NIV)** *"It was by faith that Abraham obeyed when God called him to leave home and go to another land that God would give him as his inheritance. He went without knowing where he was going."*

The decision crystallized in a moment of clarity: "Move to Kansas ,Son, as Abraham moved and embraced his new place among strangers." The choice was clear—embrace change, trust the divine plan, and begin a new chapter.

Though heavy with grief, my mind filled with hope as I prepared to enter the unknown. Guided by trust and the promise of a brighter future, I would move to Kansas to be near my children. It was a decision filled with determination and the belief in a brighter future, despite the challenges ahead.

Later, I had a serious conversation with Cindy and informed her of my resolution to leave Colorado and relocate to Kansas to be near my kids. Desiring to give her a way out, I didn't expect her to follow me as she began her career in the mountain state.

"Darlin, I love you, but I have decided to move nearer to my kids. I can't live without them. That being said, I want you to know that I don't expect you to go with me. I know that you are just starting your career here. So, this is your chance to cut and run, and there will be no ill feelings. I fully understand if you choose to stay."

Without missing a beat, she answered, "I love you too, and where you go, I will go."

After a time of courtship, we talked about marriage. If we were going to uproot our lives and move away to a new place, we should commit to each other and marry.

Aware that it might be too soon after a painful divorce, it still seemed to be the right thing to do. The next day, I began to look for job fairs. Leaving my current school was difficult because it had a state-of-the-art gymnasium, an excellent administrator, and a dynamic staff. Nevertheless, one thing inspired me: I had to be closer to my kids.

Discovering a job fair in Greeley, I arrived sicker than a desert goat on garlic but determined to find employment in Kansas. Hundreds of schools from many different states attended. However, only two school districts were hiring in Kansas: Garden City and Dodge City. The kids' mom lived with her new husband in Meade, about thirty minutes from Dodge City and about an hour from Garden City. Of course, I wanted the position nearest to my kids, but I would take whatever I could.

During the meeting, each superintendent asked, "Why Kansas? Why would you ever want to leave colorful Colorado to live in Kansas?"

After a brief explanation of the situation, I stated, "Sir, I am willing to be a Skin Diver for the Roto-Rooter Septic Company to be closer to my kids, but I would prefer to work for you."

They found that humorous, but could see my sincerity. The meeting was unique because I also had to introduce Cindy. She had a prior commitment and couldn't attend the job fair. So, I presented her resume and pitched for her as well. It was easy to brag about her because she had been a student intern under my mentorship, and I believed she would be a dynamo of an educator. She did not disappoint, as she went on to win the prestigious Horizon Award that year—an award only given to the best first-year educator in the state.

After the interviews concluded on Saturday, I felt confident and at peace.

On Monday morning, we received calls from two Principals in Dodge City, Kansas. They wanted us to come for a second interview on Thursday. Those were the days before Zoom and Facetime. Full of Godfidence, I knew this was His will, and my sister was right; everything would be okay.

In the interview, I was asked to take a position teaching Science at an at-risk school similar to Boys Town, founded by Father Flannigan. These were troubled teens with diverse abusive backgrounds.

I joyfully accepted the role, knowing it would be gratifying because of the impact I could have on these special needs kids.

Cindy was also offered a position teaching Science at the middle school. We thanked the Lord for showing us His favor and giving us jobs close to the kids!

Having secured employment, we now needed to find a suitable house. Since we were there, we decided to get a realtor and start looking. To our amazement, homes were much more affordable than in Colorado. We prayed for the right house and then began to thank Him for what He had for us. The realtor wanted to show us a beautiful residence in what once was the rich people's district.

We responded, "Thank you, but we're sure that's out of our budget range."

She insisted, "I want you to take a look. It's the ideal house for a family with young children." We hesitated but agreed.

As we entered the nostalgic neighborhood, we saw a beautiful home on a knoll surrounded by pine trees. When we pulled into the huge driveway, a basketball hoop hung, waiting for children's laughter—an in-ground swimming pool with a spacious grassy area awaited in the backyard. The house was a tri-level with a basement, garage, four bedrooms, and two baths. Downstairs, there was a game room where the kids could set up a billiard table, foosball, ping-pong, dartboard, and TV.

The agent was right; we loved the house, but now came the hard part. "Do we dare ask the cost?" This beautiful home in a quaint, quiet neighborhood would no doubt be unaffordable for us. The realtor took our breath away when she said, "How does $110,000 sound?"

"Did we hear you right? How can a home like this with all these amenities be so inexpensive? What's wrong with it?" I quipped.

The realtor assured us, "I am confident the inspection will be favorable." She also explained the difference in housing prices compared to where we had been living. We put a contract on the house and gazed Heavenward with grateful hearts. Amazed and humbled, we left town to return to our hometown to pack; we were in awe of what the Lord had done. Once again, it was a miracle from Heaven! In one day, we both got jobs and put a contract on the perfect house for our family.

It was essential to call Anna to inform her of the new plan.

"Hello, Ann; I need to tell you something that may surprise you. The kids will not have to live apart from their daddy after all."

"What do you mean?"

After explaining what God had done and how He led me to make this decision, I told her, "I just can't live without them, and I know they need me in their lives." The kids were ecstatic because they were bonded to me, and this transition had been tough for them. I have never praised God like I praised Him on that day.

The new chapter of my life with Cindy, the job opportunities, and the dream home are another reminder of God's goodness. As I share this chapter's closing lines, I sense a hunger stirring in the hearts of readers—a craving to unravel the rest of the story and witness how God's faithfulness continues to shape the unwritten pages of my life.

The journey unfolds, and I invite you to join me in the anticipation of the next chapter, where God's goodness prevails against all odds.

Photos of our Kansas home in 2003

[41]

Digital Depiction

Takeaways and Lessons Learned

1. **Faith and Resilience in Adversity:**
    - This story illustrates the power of faith and resilience in adversity. Despite the challenges of a painful divorce, a legal battle, and the potential separation from his children, the author turned to prayer and sought solace in his faith. The unexpected message from his deceased sister provided a source of hope and comfort, showing that sometimes, answers come in unexpected and miraculous ways. *The lesson here is to maintain faith during difficult times and be open to unexpected sources of support and guidance.*

[41] Tool, D. E. (2024). Kids and dogs in the pool [Digital image]. Online. OpenAI. (2024). ChatGPT (4o) [Large language model]. https://chatgpt.com/c/67956650-b0da-4db0-a561-08825e073d46

2. **Embracing Change and Trusting the Divine Plan:**
    - The author faced a significant life-changing decision: to move to Kansas and be closer to his children or resist change. Inspired by the story of Abraham's journey in the Bible, he chose to embrace the uncertainty, trust in the divine plan, and start a new chapter in his life. *This emphasizes the importance of being open to change, even when it seems daunting, and trusting that there might be a greater purpose guiding our paths.*
3. **Community and Support:**
    - The support from unexpected sources was crucial in shaping the author's journey. The phone call from his sister's friend, Tracy, who conveyed a message from beyond, provided a lifeline of encouragement. Additionally, the author's decision to involve Cindy, his former intern, in the job search and relocation process showcased the significance of building a supportive community. *The lesson learned is the value of seeking and accepting support from others during challenging times.*

Reflection Questions for Application

These questions are not just for pondering but for actively engaging in self-reflection. They are tools to help us better understand ourselves and grow from our experiences.

1. **How can I apply faith and resilience in my own life during challenging situations?**
    - Reflect on moments of difficulty and consider how faith, prayer, and resilience can be integrated into your coping mechanisms. What sources of inspiration or support can you turn to during tough times?

2. **In what areas of my life am I resistant to change, and how might embracing change lead to positive outcomes?**
    - Identify aspects of your life where you may be resistant to change. Reflect on the potential benefits of embracing change, trusting in a higher plan, and being open to new opportunities.
3. **How can I build and nurture a supportive community during significant life transitions?**
    - Consider the importance of community and support networks. Reflect on who can be part of your support system during change or difficulty. How can you cultivate and strengthen these connections to navigate challenges more effectively?

22

A Family's Journey of Faith and Liberation

"Embracing Growth, Love, and Divine Guidance from Kansas to Colorado"

Returning to the golden plains of Kansas, our family found a haven, a place of joy, and shared laughter that echoed through the walls of our new Dodge City home. Our journey unfolded like a storybook, with Wiley, the Black Lab puppy, as our faithful companion.

The weekend arrived when we introduced the kids to their new home in Dodge City. They dashed through the house and claimed their rooms with pride and joy. They couldn't wait to try the swimming pool; they splashed and laughed for hours.

"Check out this cannonball, everybody, Isaac said as he splashed water onto the rooftop."

In pure daredevil form, "Oh ya! Watch this flip," Jacob exclaimed as he twirled off the high shed into the pool.

The girls had a blast creating funny, crazy hairdos with their soaked heads.

Not to be outdone, our large labrador, Wiley, joined in the fun. He would even follow the kids onto the trampoline and diving board to jump in. When they came for a swim, this became a regular request for the kids' friends.

"Mr. Bruton, can Wiley come out to play?"

After my first year of teaching science in Kansas, a Health and Physical Education position opened up in the district. Despite the enjoyment of working with at-risk adolescents, it was an emotional rollercoaster because I would bond with students only to find them transferred to another facility without closure; this wore on me.

"That is not good for kids or you," Cindy said, with an understanding nod.

"This is not good for their learning or psychological well-being," I replied.

I applied for the transfer and was granted the Physical Education job at a 5th—and 6th-grade center.

Cindy also transferred into a Middle School Physical Education role three years later. We both found our stride.

Incredible blessings and productivity marked our decade in Kansas. I was head wrestling coach and assistant for football, gymnastics, and track and field. In contrast, Cindy's roles as the head coach for gymnastics, volleyball, and track and field allowed us to have a positive impact on the athletes under our mentorship.

For example, heartfelt conversations initiated by our athletes about God and spirituality were common on long journeys to tournaments. Many young men and women sought answers to their spiritual questions, and we embraced the task of shaping their perspectives with joy.

In a beautiful testament to the power of belief, several of the boys turned away from their involvement in street gangs and embraced the teachings of Jesus Christ. It was a privilege to lead a Bible study with these teenagers in our home, which made our time in Kansas uplifting and rewarding.

The second year in Kansas marked a pivotal point for our family. My oldest son, Isaac, wanted a more extensive high school experience and a closer connection to me and decided to live with us full-time. His enthusiasm was contagious, and my other son, Jacob, soon followed suit. They cherished their relationship with their mother, but yearned for more significant time with me and the options a larger town offered.

A short time later, my daughter, Becky joined, which completed the tribe of four now dwelling under one roof.

Every tale has a twist, and ours took an unexpected turn. One evening, while watching TV, I heard Denzel Washington Speaking to Will Smith, "Be careful, my brother. It is when all is well and you are on top that Satan comes for you!"

Denzel's words rang true. Amid our joy and success, spiritual warfare waged against our union. I found myself entangled in a temptation that threatened everything we held dear. Denzel's words reminded me of the warning in **1 Peter 5:8** (NIV): "Be alert and of sober mind. Your enemy, the devil, prowls around like a roaring lion, looking for someone to devour."

At the elementary school where I taught, a dynamic Kindergarten teacher—an attractive young lady—reached out to me for counseling due to an uncertainty about her engagement. Despite Cindy's cautions, I dismissed her concerns as silly and ignored her gut feeling, which proved a grave mistake.

"Don't be silly, sweetheart. I am twenty years older than her, happily married, and we are just colleagues."

Believing that the young woman could be attracted to me, Cindy cautioned, "I have a gut feeling that she might be attracted to you. Please be careful."

The thought was dismissed as absurd.

A word of caution: Friends, do not ignore your parents' or wife's instincts; it is a safeguard that must not be overlooked.

Subsequent sessions led to conversations and advice, always with my office door open. However, there was a moment of weakness during our third meeting. The young lady asked for a hug, which escalated into a kiss on my neck, and I didn't resist. It was nothing more than a kiss, but the aftermath brought swift remorse as the gravity of my actions swallowed me like a hungry lion.

The only path to protecting my marriage was through immediate honesty and accountability to Cindy without delay.

The next day, I took Cindy to breakfast, and I mustered the courage to reveal my transgression.

"Darlin, I have something to tell you, and it will not be easy for either of us," I said, embarrassed by my weakness.

The conversation began, and I explained the situation in detail and apologized for not heeding her advice. Understandably, her initial response was one of hurt and anger.

"I told you!" came her reply through tears and gritted teeth.

She asked questions to clarify the details and thanked me for not letting it go any further. At first, I questioned the wisdom of my decision to share the painful truth. Still, I soon realized that transparency was essential for the healing to begin.

This lack of judgment, letting my guard down, and ignoring my wife's caution caused much pain. But had I not been forthcoming, it could have been disastrous.

Despite the challenges, God's goodness prevailed. Our commitment to each other and our convictions helped us navigate the storm and rebuild what had been damaged. Through the dark times and the scars left by that mistake, I encountered the depth of forgiveness, grace, and the power of redemption that only Jesus can provide. Our story is a testament to the resilience of the human spirit and the hope that even in the darkest times, redemption is possible.

Although our years in Kansas were full of joy and fulfillment, this legacy book would only be complete if I acknowledged the trials we faced and the lessons we learned during those years.

In a three-year period, a significant transition occurred. Our children graduated from high school and embarked on their own paths. Isaac made the courageous choice to join the army and was dedicated to serving his country. Jacob returned to the Rocky Mountains and sought uncharted possibilities. My daughter, Becky, entered a sacred headlock—oops, I mean wedlock—and my stepdaughter, Janelle, went to Fort Collins to train as an RN nurse.

With this pivotal juncture, the sense that it was time to return home to Colorado solidified in our hearts. Guided by our trust in the Almighty, we began a period of prayer and pursued teaching positions in our beautiful home state. Our aspirations aligned when we discovered a Physical Education position open in a quaint mountain town connected to Cindy's roots—her birthplace and childhood home. They needed a female teacher. Therefore, driven by providence, Cindy applied for the position. Within a week, the call came.

"Hello, Mrs. Bruton. We have received your application and very impressive resume. We want to schedule an interview with you this Friday. Can you do that?" They offered.

"Yes, absolutely. Thank you for contacting me and allowing me to display my experience and qualifications to enhance your students' learning. I look forward to meeting you," Cindy said with an excited countenance.

The interview was successful, and she was offered the job. However, uncertainty lingered because only one job was secured. Trusting in the Lord's guidance, I visited the university to introduce myself to the Exercise Sports Science department administrative chair.

In a providential encounter, we connected like battery cables. The encounter revealed a potential full-time professorship on the horizon and an immediate need for an Adjunct professor. The subjects included Health and Wellness, Biomechanics, Kinesiology, Sports Law, and Methods courses, which aligned with my professional expertise.

God's hand was evident as He straightened the crooked road and smoothed the path before us. With provision in place, we searched for a home to rent with an option to buy. We discovered a rustic house high on a hill. The air was fresh and clean, and it overlooked a green valley full of cattle grazing and majestic mountains in the background—a dream come true. The view itself was worth a million dollars. The rent was fair and budget-friendly.

Once again, our Heavenly Father helped us secure employment in our professions and led us to the perfect house all in one day.

With the prospect of returning to our Colorado homeland in mind, we faced the challenge of selling our Kansas home during a severe housing crisis in 2009. Holding steadfast faith, we drew strength from past experiences of God's miraculous provision. I recalled how the Lord had facilitated the sale of my first house within an hour and the farm in just three days; we embarked on this endeavor with Godfidence.

We needed to set a one-month window for selling our spacious family abode in Kansas because our jobs in Colorado would begin in August. Despite naysayers, we took a leap of faith and listed it as "For Sale by Owner."

Colorful balloons and eye-catching advertisements drew attention to its unique charm. Two days after I posted a flyer in my school's teachers' lounge, I received a phone call, which led to a divine connection.

A colleague's enthusiastic interest prompted a viewing with his wife, who loved the house and its various attractions for a family. However, their eagerness hinged on the selling of their own home. There was concern because they had listed it for six months the previous year without success, and there was not even one showing.

The eager partners were informed about our time constraint and that we could not make a contingent contract. Wanting to be encouraging, I said, "We will pray that you get a buyer soon, and then we can seal the deal."

The couple were also Christians, and they joined us in that prayer. Their new realtor came on Saturday and put up the signs. On Monday, the realtor called them and wanted to show the house to a pre-approved interested party.

The investor put a contract on their residence on Tuesday. Both transactions proceeded with remarkable smoothness, defying the economic challenges of the time. The original price of our Kansas property was $110,000, and it now sold for an astounding $165,000 during a recession year. The purchase was a testament to God's intervention and ability to control outcomes that far exceed human expectations.

With our trucks packed to the brim, we began the trip back to Colorado. One of our trucks was so heavy that it looked like an ant lifting a lifesaver. We were greeted by a fortunate occurrence when we arrived at our new home. There just happened to be a summer wrestling camp in Gunnison, our new town. Many of my former Kansas wrestlers were attending that camp. What were the chances?

The morning after we arrived, ten muscular lads helped us unload. Their presence reminded us of the Father's orchestrations beyond our comprehension.

In reflection, the Lord's unending goodness marked every step of our journey. His providence shone through every chapter of our story, from the small town that mirrored Cindy's roots to the job opportunities and the divine synchronicity of home sales. The road back to Colorado was paved with signs of grace, affirming the truth of **Isaiah 45:2:** "He went before us and made the rough places smooth and the crooked places straight."

As we settled into our new mountain residence, we greeted this fresh season with joy and again stood in awe of God's faithfulness and guiding hand.

[42]

Working it out and moving forward.
Digital depiction

[42] Tool, E. E. (2024, July 28). Mark's Transparency With Cindy. Chat GPT 4.0. Retrieved July 28, 2024, from https://chatgpt.com/c/2df683d1-66f3-41a7-9070-85070b7f8481

[43] Digital depiction of:
Mark's remorse and transparency

Takeaways and Lessons Learned:

1. **Navigating Challenges with Faith:**
   The narrative underscores the importance of facing life's challenges with faith and trust in God. Despite unexpected turns and personal failings, the family experienced God's grace and redemption by relying on their faith.
2. **Transparency and Accountability:**
   The story highlights the vital role of transparency and accountability in personal relationships. Despite the consequences, the author's immediate honesty with his spouse led to healing and restoration. It emphasizes the value of open communication, especially during difficult times. Mark guarded himself from the enemy's attack by being transparent with Cindy immediately.

---

[43] Bruton, M. W. TOOL, D. E. (2024, June 25). Pushing Through and Moving Forward. Chat GPT 4.0. Retrieved June 25, 2024, from https://chatgpt.com/c/ba895eaf-f18e-4ea7-aea7-3a169f6d581f

3. **Divine Guidance in Life Transitions:**
   The family's journey reveals a pattern of divine guidance in significant life transitions. From job opportunities aligning perfectly, to the timely sale of their home, the story suggests that trusting in God's providence can lead to unexpected blessings even in the face of uncertainty.

Reflection Questions for Application:

1. How do you approach challenges and uncertainties in your life? What role does your faith play in navigating complex situations?
2. Consider a moment in your life where transparency and accountability were crucial in resolving a conflict or overcoming an obstacle. How did this experience shape your relationships?
3. Reflect on a significant life transition or decision. Were there signs of divine guidance or unexpected blessings that influenced the outcome? How can you incorporate trust in God's providence into your decision-making process?

23

Divine U-Turns

Navigating Unexpected Paths and Embracing New Beginnings

We nestled into our charming mountain town, heart's content, and at peace. One evening, gazing over the valley below, we admired the green fields and majestic mountains bathed in the sunset's warm and colorful hues. A shared glance between us conveyed it all.

"We're not in Kansas anymore," we chuckled as we acknowledged this fresh chapter. Our smiles were so broad that we looked like we had swallowed a communion rail.

Life, much like a novel, never follows a predictable course. Cindy thrived in her new roles as an athletic director, physical education teacher, and coach for various sports. She had the energy of a hummingbird on caffeine; she juggled track and field, cross country, and gymnastics. Drawn back into coaching, I joined the high school staff to coach wrestling and found joy in assisting the gymnastics team.

Despite life's gentle ebb, my part-time university professor role fell short of our financial needs. A rumor about a remarkable church seeking a new pastor reached me. The former senior minister often invited me to be his guest speaker in his absence—a privilege.

Applying for this role would be daunting due to my past mistakes, particularly my separation from Ann. Yet, the prospect of preaching, teaching, leading, inspiring, and guiding resonated deep within me—an intrinsic calling etched into my very being.

However, a sense of unworthiness cloaked me. In a prayer that echoed my uncertainty, I conversed with my Heavenly Father, "Lord, if this is Your will, then I will ***not*** submit my resume unless they contact me first."

If asked to submit my resume, and in the spirit of truth, disclosing my divorce from Ann upfront would be vital. If they still wanted me, I would be assured that it was God's will for me to take the pastorate and also keep my university professorship.

My phone rang the next day; it was one of the church leaders. "Mr. Bruton, would you please consider applying for our pastoral position?"

"Thank you for your call, brother. But, before I answer, I would like to meet for coffee to discuss a few things that I think are important for you to know and are necessary for all of us to make the right decision with the Lord's blessing."

We met that afternoon, and I explained my divorce situation and answered a few preliminary questions. After the leadership team convened, the Elders said they were unified and wanted me to apply. This meeting was a pivotal moment in my journey.

The synchronicity of my prayer and this call stirred within me a significant realization. Despite my failures and past scars, I sensed a tug and an unmistakable nudge that affirmed this was my path. The Holy Spirit also reminded me of the many men and women in the Bible that God continued to use even after their colossal failures. The choice was as clear as a shimmering beacon on a hill, guiding my steps forward, and it filled me with a profound sense of divine guidance.

With a deep sense of humility, a profound hope, and the assurance that divine goodness directed my life, I embraced my destiny.

It is ironic that I was offered the *pastor* position at the same time a **full-time** opening at the university was offered. The professorship had allure and paid more, but the magnetic pull of purpose and a higher calling steered me like a GPS. I chose to shepherd the flock of this dynamic little congregation.

When I assumed leadership of the small, yet vibrant assembly, our gatherings occurred in a cozy coffee shop. It was no larger than a postage stamp, a bit dark, and always smelled of fresh-brewed coffee, but the room was our weekly haven. We rearranged chairs and tables every week to create a semblance of a cozy gathering place.

This arrangement had been the norm for years. Still, a whisper in my heart, reminiscent of Moses leading the Israelites out of Egypt, urged me to consider more spacious horizons. After I had been there for a year, I felt led by the Holy Spirit; I believed the time had come to find a suitable worship space—a warm, inviting, and more sacred place.

I began an earnest prayer journey without divulging a word to the congregation. I sought divine guidance for our church's future. Memories of a picturesque Seventh-day Adventist church atop a gentle hill outside our town flickered in my mind.

The Holy Spirit prompted me to visit the quaint building and pray. I remembered that the sanctuary had an emerald green carpet, polished oak pews, a fellowship hall, a kitchen, Sunday school rooms, a pastor's office, and a prominent moss rock baptismal, contributing to an atmosphere of peace and tranquility.

While I sat in my truck in the parking lot, I said a specific prayer and asked the Lord for divine guidance. "Father, could this be the place where our congregation would flourish? Could we, in unity, share this hallowed space? Heavenly Father, please show me where we are supposed to be. For your glory, in Jesus' name. Amen!"

As I drove away, I was filled with excitement and wonder, and pondered what God might do. Ten minutes later, while I was driving home, an unexpected call disrupted my thoughts—an old high school classmate, now a prominent figure in the Seventh-day Adventist community, had a proposal.

"Hey Mark, How's it going, brother? This is Dale. I hear good things about your church. The leadership team and I would like to propose an offer to you."

I was smiling like a coyote at a rabbit convention, wondering if this was the Lord's answer already.

"Sure, partner; I'm all ears."

"Our congregation has been dwindling, and we can't pay our bills. I know you are not Seventh-day Adventists, but we would like to rent the building to your church. We meet on Saturdays, and you could use the building on Sundays."

The timing between their proposal and my prayer was uncanny, but the rental cost would be the clincher since our group had only paid a mere $600 a month for the coffee shop. Sensing that the Lord's plan was already beginning to unfold, I asked,

"How much is your leadership team asking per month, brother?"

"How does $600 a month sound?"

"I need to run it by my congregation and the leadership team, but it sounds like a divine plan might be coming together. Thank you for considering us. We will be in touch."

I also told him about my visit to the property and my prayer. We chuckled at the goodness of our Father in Heaven.

An overwhelming sense of divine intervention washed over me. God had answered my prayer with astonishing speed—a clear sign of His providence and leading.

Excitement bubbled within me as I contemplated the open door before us. The hand of God was evident, guiding us through this unexpected avenue.

When our congregation gathered the following Sunday, I shared the astounding news. We were journeying toward our promised land—the charming chapel on the hill. Joy lit up their faces and reflected gratitude for our Good Shepherd's unmistakable guidance.

Weeks turned into months and months into years, and we witnessed a transformation within our fellowship. Our numbers swelled, and the vitality of our church community grew exponentially.

Abundant blessings and unprecedented spiritual growth manifested—a testament to the power of prayer and God's intricate plan.

The years spent there yielded a fruitful harvest. Many people gave their lives to Christ and were baptized, and discipleship flourished. Despite the joy of being a pastor again, the calling came with a cost.

Unending hours of prayer and study, weddings, funerals, visits to the sick and hospitalized, prison Bible studies, and nursing home visits filled my days. In-home Bible studies, family counseling, and more enriched the ministry, but burned me out. Beneath the surface, I wrestled with the unrelenting pressure to embody perfection.

Congregants often place pastors on a pedestal, demanding flawless devotion. Some churches raise the bar so high for their pastors that even Jesus cannot reach it.

Against this backdrop, my union with Cindy began to unravel, which resurfaced broken trust from my involvement in that forbidden kiss with a co-worker years prior. Though it happened long ago, Cindy's pain remained raw. It was always there like a coiled cobra.

One Sunday morning, an unexpected reunion with an old classmate reignited memories. She lived in Denver, was visiting the Western slope, and attended our service on her way to her family in a distant town. Nostalgic after forty years, our conversation about her husband's tragic death led to a brief interaction. Due to a prior commitment, I had to end the discussion abruptly. Later, I felt guilty for this abrupt ending and reached out to her during the week to apologize.

She was the first girl I dated in high school in 1977. We reconnected on social media and reminisced about the "good old days." Our dialogue remained primarily innocent, but I made a few flirty comments about days gone by. Though she knew I was jesting, I shouldn't have said those things.

When Cindy saw the comments, she misinterpreted them and retreated inside herself. I am not minimizing her feelings because I had already broken her trust once before.

Cindy's swift emotional withdrawal resembled a brush fire with high winds. She moved into another room and withheld physical and emotional intimacy due to mounting pain and distrust. The incident ripped a scab off an old wound.

I sought resolution through regular counseling for us in a distant town. As a pastor, you are not allowed to admit marital trouble. This would mean you are imperfect and, therefore, not worthy of the position. Sessions yielded little progress and deepened the gulf between us.

What seemed like a slight misunderstanding to me became a storm of emotions and fears for Cindy. A year of silence and exclusion took its toll and drove us further apart. My son saw the painful effect it had on me and tried to intervene by writing her a letter:

"Cindy, you are doing the exact opposite of what you should do if you want to save your marriage. To salvage your relationship, it would help if you stopped the silent treatment and rejection." Jacob's attempt to intervene was brushed aside.

Faced with relentless negation and the burden of mending the irreparable, I reached a crossroads. The effort to save our partnership and to be the perfect pastor drained my soul.

Despite my best efforts, our marriage crumbled. Unable to navigate the line between executing the duties of a pastor and being human, I resigned.

A heavy darkness descended, and depression claimed me. The sense of failure overwhelmed me—I felt as if I had failed not only Cindy, but also God, the church, and the community that held me in high regard.

Engulfed in a sea of shadows, I found myself in despair. In one week, I put down two cherished dogs who had grown old and ill, resigned from a job I loved and income, lost my sense of purpose, and said goodbye to another fifteen-year marriage. It was a perfect storm with a black sky, lightning strikes, and high waves billowing in my soul. I began to sink fast. Yet, beneath the raging sea were God's everlasting and ever-merciful arms, pulling me back to the surface.

This chapter testifies that life's journey includes both peaks and valleys. The legacy I sought to write isn't just a rosy recollection of sunshine and rainbows but an honest account of the struggles, doubts, and failures that define my humanity.

During this deep darkness, God's goodness remained a glimmer of hope on the horizon—a light I clung to with unrelenting faith even in my darkest hours. However, questions cried out in my mind: "Now, what will He do with me? Is my life over? Will I wander like a fugitive as a 'has been'?"

Little did I know that God would close this chapter of my life and open a new one that would outshine them all. My Heavenly Father still loved me and had a purpose for my life.

My dissolution of marriage, without a doubt, broke His heart, but He didn't throw me away. It is important to know that people will give up on you, but God never will.

While fighting the demons of rejection, I found a song that helped anchor me: "**Tell Your Heart to Beat Again.**" [44] Written by Bernie Herms, Randy Phillips, and Mathew West. To the broken-hearted warriors, I recommend you listen to it if you are in a dark place.

---

[44] Goke, D., Phillips, R., Herms, B., & West, M. (2014, January 5). About Tell Your Heart to Beat Again. Lyrics. Retrieved June 24, 2023, from
https://www.lyrics.com/lyric/30872913/Tell+Your+Heart+to+Beat+Again

Takeaways and Lessons Learned:

Embrace God's Love and Forgiveness: The story highlights how God's grace, love, and forgiveness are ever-present, even in the face of failures and mistakes. Despite the author's past errors, God's divine guidance and intervention show that His grace is abundant and unending.

1. **Persevere Through Trials:** The narrative underscores the importance of not giving up when faced with challenges, struggles, and even failures. The authors' journey showcases the resilience required to navigate the twists and turns of life, leaning on faith to overcome adversity.
2. **God's Plans Surpass Human Understanding:** The story illustrates how God's plans often exceed human expectations. Despite doubts and uncertainties, the writers' path unfolds unexpectedly, leading to new beginnings far surpassing what was initially perceived as possible.

Reflection Questions for Application:

1. How can I embrace and internalize the concept of God's unconditional love and forgiveness in my own life, particularly when facing my shortcomings and mistakes?
2. How can I draw strength from the writers' example and perseverance to keep moving forward and trusting in God's guiding hand when confronted with challenges, setbacks, or failures?
3. How can I cultivate a deeper understanding of God's plans for me, recognizing that His direction might lead to outcomes beyond my current comprehension? How can I develop the patience and faith to await His perfect timing?

24

Falling Forward

Discovering God's Grace Through the Flaws of Biblical Characters

Pastor Levi Lusko shares a tender story about collecting shells on the beach with his daughter, Clover. As Levi sought only perfect, intact shells, Clover was drawn to the broken ones. When her little hands could hold no more, she turned to her father and declared, "Daddy, the broken ones are beautiful, too." This simple yet profound truth mirrors how God views us. He sees the beauty in our brokenness and has the power to transform us.

The late Pastor Adrian Rogers said, "Men throw broken things away, but God never uses anything until He first breaks it."

After Cindy and I separated, I found myself in a deep ocean and struggled to stay afloat. I felt like one of those fractured shells tossed about by the waves. In my desperation, I turned to God's Word for guidance. The Bible is not just a book of stories; it's a testament to the transformative power of God's grace. It's rich with stories of triumph, redemption, and faith, but it also contains accounts of failure and imperfection.

Like the shattered shells on the beach, these stories remind us that we are still beautiful in God's eyes, even in our brokenness.

Have you ever felt like a failure, convinced that your mistakes have disqualified you from achieving anything meaningful? That is what Ole' Forky-tail wants us to believe. Imagine the mistakes that haunt you, becoming the stepping stones to your greatest triumphs.

In the Bible, it's not the flawless characters who make the most impact but those who stumble, falter, and fail. These are the individuals God uses in a mighty way to shape history and fulfill His divine purposes. As you read this chapter, prepare to be inspired and encouraged by the profound truth that your blunders do not define you—God's grace does.

Their stories are a testament to the fact that our failures, far from the end of our story, can become the stairs to our most significant accomplishments.

I want to lead you through the stories that strengthened me when I became discouraged and wondered if God would ever use me again.

Sometimes, we elevate Bible characters to the status of heroes, forgetting that they, too, grappled with their own imperfections and vulnerabilities, much like we do. It's astonishing to observe the multitude of these "great lives" that were men and women who contended with personal struggles and weighty family difficulties and dysfunctions just as we do.

The book of Hebrews in the New Testament showcases remarkable men and women who demonstrated strong faith and received God's blessings and favor. You will be intrigued to see how these people, despite their imperfections, played a significant role in God's plans.

What adds to the intrigue is that chapter 11 of Hebrews highlights their successes but omits their mistakes and failures that helped make them who they are. Perhaps this could be attributed to God's perspective, which focuses on our potential in Christ rather than our shortcomings.

The relatability of these characters should serve as a comforting reminder that we are not alone in our struggles.

I don't know about you, but I gain enormous encouragement from this fact. It does not serve as a validation for wrongdoing or unhealthy conduct. Still, it does present a comforting representation of the challenges intrinsic to the human journey. It is reassuring to recognize that I'm not alone in dealing with such issues, and neither are you. Let's look at just a few of them:

Adam and Eve: The First Failures

Adam and Eve, our first ancestors, were created perfect and had direct communication with God. Yet, they disobeyed God by eating the forbidden fruit, bringing sin into the world. Their story highlights that even in a perfect environment, humans can fail. Parents, take heart; even God's flawless parenting and ideal circumstances did not prevent His children from going astray.

King Saul: The Jealous King

Saul, chosen for his handsome and large appearance, started as a humble king who loved God. However, pride, jealousy, and disobedience led to his downfall. Ignoring God's command, he spared the Amalekite king and livestock, causing God to reject him as king, which led to his suicide.

"Why have you disobeyed the Lord's command?" Samuel confronted Saul after the battle with the Amalekites.

"I did obey," Saul insisted. "I spared Agag and took the best sheep and cattle."

Samuel's stern reply cut through Saul's excuses, "To obey is better than sacrifice."

Saul's story teaches us that disobedience and pride have serious consequences.

David: A Man after God's Own Heart

David is celebrated for his bravery and faith, especially in his battle against Goliath. However, his life went astray when he committed adultery with Bathsheba and arranged her husband's murder to cover his sin. When confronted by Nathan, the prophet, David's heart broke with repentance.

"Why did you despise the word of the Lord by doing what is evil in His eyes?" Nathan asked.

"I have sinned against the Lord," David admitted, showing deep remorse.

His heartfelt prayer in Psalm 51 reveals his genuine repentance and highlights God's grace in his restoration. The Lord went on to use him in mighty ways.

Solomon: The Wisest King

Solomon, known for his wisdom and wealth, defied God's law by marrying many foreign women, leading him into idolatry. His obsession with wealth and power resulted in significant mistakes. In the end, Solomon realized that true happiness comes only by living for the Eternal King, not material possessions.

Samson: The He-Man with a She Weakness:

Samson's strength came from his obedience to God, not his long hair. His infatuation with Philistine women led to his downfall. Because of his disobedience, he lost his strength and sight, but he repented, and God restored his strength to defeat Israel's enemies. His story highlights the dangers of yielding to temptation and God's readiness to restore us when we repent. This should reassure us that no matter how far we've strayed, God is always ready to welcome us back with open arms.

Moses: The Reluctant Leader

Moses was a murderer and stuttered. He spent 40 years thinking he was somebody, 40 years finding out that he was a nobody, and then 40 years finding out what God could do with a nobody. The Almighty used him to lead Israel out of Egypt despite his reluctance and many faults. His story emphasizes that even great leaders can make mistakes, but God's grace remains sufficient.

Noah: The Patient Builder

Noah's faithfulness stands out as he spent 120 years building the ark and preaching repentance. However, he fell into drunkenness after the flood. Noah's story teaches us that past faithfulness doesn't prevent future mistakes, but consistent obedience to God is crucial.

Peter: The Church Leader

Peter, known for his temper and cursing, denied Jesus three times but repented, became the disciples' leader, and delivered the initial evangelistic message, saving over 3,000 individuals (Acts 2:14-36).

Peter finished strong and was crucified upside down on a cross for his faith.

His transformation demonstrates that failure doesn't disqualify us from God's plans.

Jonah: The Reluctant Prophet

Jonah initially refused to obey God and ran from his mission. But after becoming fish food, he repented and ultimately obeyed.

"In my distress, I called to the Lord, and He answered me," Jonah prayed.

This story reminds us that God withdraws His judgment on the sinner who repents and asks for His forgiveness. Jonah went on to accomplish the mission that God gave him.

Abraham: The Father of Faith

Abraham, the Father of the Jewish people, made big mistakes, like lying about his wife and nearly getting her raped, twice. His son, Isaac, did the same thing. At the insistence of Sarah, Abraham also slept with her handmaid, Hagar. Sarah began to doubt that the Lord would keep his promise of giving them a child in their old age, so she took matters into her own hands and sent Abraham to the neighbor girl's house.

However, in her defense, we don't see where Abraham disagreed with her advice either. He was on that young lady's doorstep in two flips of a lamb's ear. The consequence of this one-night stand was Ishmael, the Father of the Arab nation. Abraham was a great man of God, but far from perfect. He was very human, just like you and me. His story underscores that God's promises stand despite our mistakes.

"Look up at the sky and count the stars—if indeed you can count them," God told Abraham, reaffirming His promise.

Isaac: Favoritism and lies

Isaac favored his eldest son, Esau, but this proved fatal within the family relationship. His bias almost cost the lives of both sons, Esau and Jacob. Isaac obeyed God's call and lived a long, faithful life despite his mistakes.

Jacob: The Deceiver Turned Israel

Jacob deceived and manipulated his father to gain Esau's birthright, leading to years of strife. Wrestling with God marked his transformation.

"I will not let you go unless you bless me," Jacob insisted during the struggle.

The Lord renamed him Israel, signifying his changed heart and renewed faith.

His story teaches the importance of facing our mistakes and seeking God's blessing.

The Prodigal Son: The Return Home

The prodigal son is a household name for every family member who is considered a "black sheep." Lured away by wealth, the young man left home to spend his inheritance. He lived a sinful life of lavish extravagance until all his fortune and hope were spent.

The story of this wayward son reminds us that worldly happiness is only temporary. Some people may only appear to care for us when we are successful but desert us when we are lost.

A repentant sinner, the wanderer returned to his Father and begged forgiveness rather than continue living in misery.

"Father, I have sinned against heaven and you; please forgive me," he confessed.

I believe his father patiently waited at the window every day. Finally, he saw his son coming up the road looking like a gutter rat in a tunic and smelling like a pig pen.

The father ran to meet him. He embraced, forgave, and restored his son by reminding him that he could do nothing to lose his father's love or sonship. There are two important lessons we can learn from this story:

1. Never let the things money can buy rob you of what money cannot buy.
2. **God is not mad at you!** He is longing for you to return to Him. But He will never force you. He will let the circumstances of your poor decisions take their toll on you until you return to Him. When you do, your Heavenly Father will greet you with open arms. He won't make you earn your way back. Jesus already did that for us. We must turn from our sin and reckless ways, and He will welcome us home and give us purpose again.

The Samaritan Woman: From Adultery to Evangelist

She had five husbands and was almost stoned to death for committing adultery. Jesus intervened and did not condemn her like the **religious** leaders. Despite her sinful past, Jesus' conversation with this woman led to her transformation and evangelistic zeal.

"He told me everything I ever did," she proclaimed, leading many to believe in Jesus.

Her story shows that no past is too tarnished for God's redemption.

King Hezekiah: The Prideful Reformer

Hezekiah's pride in displaying his wealth led to the prophecy of the Babylonian exile. Yet, his faith saved Judah from Assyria.

"Because you have prayed to me, I have heard you," God assured through Isaiah.

Hezekiah's story teaches us to trust God and repent from pride.

We must recognize our mistakes and repent when we have sinned. God's forgiveness doesn't save us from the consequences of our conduct. However, if we have abandoned the behavior and are willing to accept the results, God will still use us.

These are only a few great Bible characters who failed miserably; there are many more. It is crucial that we do not just read through these biblical accounts but that we learn from them. May these lessons on failure in the Bible encourage us, keep us rooted in Scripture, and help us keep God at the center of our lives.

"Who are they on the heights?
Are they the ones who never
Faltered nor went astray?
Nay! They who stand where
First comes dawn are those who
Stumbled, but then went on." [45]

— (Author unknown)

---

[45] Cowman, L. (2008). Poem: They On The Heights. Streams in The Desert. Zondervan. https://www.christianity.com/devotionals/streams-in-the-desert/

[46]

Takeaways or Lessons to Learned:

1. God's grace covers **all** mistakes and failures.
2. No one is too far gone or the failure too big for God to handle.
3. Grace and redemption depend not on you or your actions but on God alone.
4. God can use your biggest failures for His glory.
5. The Lord will reveal His plan and purpose for your life if you seek Him.
6. Wisdom comes from God alone. We must continue to seek the Lord and follow His lead.

---

[46] TOOL, D. E. (2024). Bible Characters Who Failed but Were Used by God [Digital depiction]. Online. https://chatgpt.com/c/10410378-2528-4ae0-be6e-61a2e6563765

7. Repentance and obedience to God is necessary to move forward.
8. No one is immune to the luring and trappings of sin and failure.
9. Disobedience to God has consequences.
10. God can and will radically change the lives of those who believe in Him.

How to move forward from failure:

Return to the Lord:

Trust that God's grace will wipe away all of your sins and mistakes. You must seek His face and confess your sins and struggles to the Lord with a humble heart. Then, turn away from your sins as you ask the Lord to help you overcome the strongholds in your life. You are never too far from God; His steadfast love pleads with you to come home.

Reflection Questions for Applying the Lessons:

1. How have you experienced God's grace covering your own mistakes and failures in the past, and what can you do to trust in His grace more fully in your present challenges?
2. Reflect on a time when you felt like your failures were insurmountable. How can you remind yourself that no failure is too big for God to handle, and what steps can you take to surrender these failures to Him?
3. Consider your understanding of grace and redemption. How can you deepen your reliance on God's grace rather than your efforts and actions, and how might this change your approach to overcoming failures and mistakes?

25

"From Crossroads to Classroom: A Journey of Rediscovery and Purpose

God's Timing and Direction Amidst Uncertainty and Despair.

Living in a borrowed camper might sound like the opening scene of a country song, but let me assure you, the chorus was far from uplifting. My soul drifted in a sea of uncertainty, a wanderer searching for purpose. Questions loomed like storm clouds: Where do I go from here? Which path should I take? Stranded at life's crossroads, I grappled for direction, **feeling the weight of despair as it pressed down on me**.

In 2015, my path ahead was shrouded in darkness. Desperate, I turned to my Heavenly Father and sought divine guidance for my life's direction. The road ahead appeared foggy and indistinct, yet I could sense the presence of the Holy Spirit, guiding me through the bleak alternative of succumbing to despair; I couldn't abandon hope.

"Get up, Mark, square your shoulders back, and hold your head high," I told myself. "Your best days are still ahead of you. You must believe that."

During a period of deep introspection, a significant blessing entered my life—a long-lost friend emerged from the shadows of time. Their presence became a beacon of timely companionship, offering wisdom and counsel when I needed it most. One evening, over coffee, I confided in them. "I don't know where to go from here. Everything seems so unclear." Their response would change my life.

"Have you considered a return to teaching?" my friend asked, their eyes searching mine.

"A little, but I'm not sure if it's the right path," I replied, feeling the weight of my uncertainty. "It is mandatory to renew my teaching license, which is no easy task."

They leaned closer, their voice steady and reassuring. "Mark, you light up when you talk about your former students. You have a gift, and it would be a shame not to share it." Their words sparked a glimmer of hope within me, and as our conversation continued, they unearthed a hidden truth about my passion that had eluded me until then.

Those words struck a chord within me, and as our conversation continued, they unearthed a hidden truth about my passion that had eluded me until then.

During our dialogues, this friend perceived a distinctive facet of my character—a deep-seated commitment to the art of teaching. They highlighted the rarity of my energy and enthusiasm, even at my age. I have been privileged to impart knowledge in this field for three decades. As an elementary Physical Education teacher, I call myself a "Funsichologist."

My friend observed how my essence ignited with a radiant glow when recounting the impactful moments and enduring impressions I crafted among my students over the years.

"You have something special," my friend continued, their voice filled with conviction. "Your passion for teaching is unmatched. You belong in the classroom, where you can shape children's lives and guide them toward health and well-being."

In a moment of profound clarity, this cherished friend ignited a spark within my soul. "You belong with children; they need you, and you need them!" My friend's declaration echoed and cast a new light on my path forward.

Inspired by this dear friend's continual encouragement and confronted by the undeniable truth they had illuminated, I resolved to renew my teaching license and update my education. The timing of this intervention was unmistakable; it was orchestrated by God. It stood as a testament to His divine grace and guided my steps in the direction that aligned with His greater purpose.

As I reflect upon this pivotal juncture, I am reminded of the Lord's boundless goodness in pre-planning the arrival of specific individuals in our lives at a precise and appointed time. Their consistent affirmation kindled a fire within my soul. It propelled me back to the realm of education, where I belong. I am filled with gratitude for their timely intervention.

With a heart that brims with gratitude, I praise God for the intricate brush strokes He uses to paint our life journeys.

However, one minor concern remained—my age! At fifty-five, re-entering the educational arena seemed like a daunting task. While I still almost have the energy and stamina I did in my thirties, the system hesitates to welcome seasoned professionals with higher degrees, fearing the weight of higher salaries. But I was not deterred.

Full of "Godfidence," I set out on the adventure to resurrect my teaching license—a necessary key to unlock doors in public education. With six postgraduate hours as my compass, I navigated the terrain of coursework, reigniting the flame of enthusiasm for teaching.

In the interim, I embraced a part-time construction job—a gritty yet invigorating endeavor that rekindled my vitality. The physical labor and team camaraderie provided a refreshing change from the academic pursuits. After three months of courses, my educational arsenal became fortified. So, I submitted my application for a renewed Colorado teaching license.

After hitting send on my certification application, I began to peruse various school district websites for potential health and physical education opportunities, even in the cozy corners of my tiny hometown of Delta, Colorado. Delta is a "poke-and-plumb town; by the time you poke your head out the window, you are plumb out of town." The city limit and exit signs are written on the same pole. But it was a wonderful place to grow up.

I also searched for the district's salary rates for substitute teachers. Many people get hired to teach by first being substitutes. They fill in for an absent educator for a much lower salary and begin to network their teaching skills and ability to build rapport with students.

As I prayed and searched online, my eyes widened. "Look at this," I murmured. "An opening for a full-time elementary physical education teaching position." What felt like a distant dream now seemed tangible, a prospect aligned with my goal.

With a heart of determination, I crafted the three-hour teacher application. As I clicked "send," I sensed a surge of anticipation and excitement. "What if it all comes together that fast?" I imagined.

Life often delivers the unexpected. It is typical for a district to take a couple of weeks to respond to a teaching application. These jobs are almost always filled within the district, but posted just to satisfy the legalities and ethics. However, my thinking was, what can it hurt? I left it in God's hands.

After working in construction all day, I smelled like a dead squirrel in a heating duct, and needed a shower. I was gone for about thirty minutes. When I returned, I noticed that I had a missed call notification, and they left a message. It was the principal behind the vacancy, extending an invitation for an interview the next day.

"Talk about perfect timing!" I exclaimed to the empty room. The Lord whispered to my heart, "I told you I will make a way for you. I am still behind the scenes, controlling the scenes that I am behind."

As I stepped into the interview room, an instant connection sparked between me, the principal, and the assistant administrator. We exchanged greetings, and the principal leaned forward. "So, tell us about your experience with BAL-A-VIS-X and Neuroscience as it applies to learning."

"These methods have been transformative in my teaching approach. They help students improve their bilateral coordination, balance, auditory, and visual skills, which are crucial for learning."

Their eyes lit up with interest, and the assistant principal nodded. "We need someone with your experience, background, and enthusiasm."

When the interview concluded, I walked away with hope and uncertainty intermingling in my thoughts. In about thirty minutes, I received a call. The administrator wanted me to return to the school. Excitement coursed through me as I hurried back.

The words I yearned for materialized—they were as excited as I was. They offered me the health and physical education position and handed me my keys.

"Welcome aboard!" the principal said, shaking my hand. It is somewhat ironic that I received the position before my license was renewed. A tidal wave of gratitude engulfed me; it was once again a testament to divine orchestration.

This chapter is but the overture to a symphony of wonder. The story's melody continues, with more breathtaking notes waiting to be played.

[47]

Takeaways or Lessons Learned:

- **Divine Timing: Trusting God's Orchestration**
  Through life's uncertainties and challenges, the author learned that God's timing is impeccable. When things seem darkest, He brings the right people and opportunities into our lives to guide us toward our purpose. Trusting His orchestration, even when we can't see the whole picture, allows us to move forward with hope and faith.
- **Unveiling Hidden Passions: Embracing Personal Uniqueness**
  The rediscovery of Mark's passion for teaching, facilitated by a dear friend's insight, reminded him that each of us possesses unique gifts and qualities that make us valuable contributors to the world. Embracing our distinctive attributes and

---

[47] Bruton, M. W. TOOL, D. E. Interview and Job Offer [Digital depiction]. Online. https://chatgpt.com/c/175b167a-c53b-451b-a539-3adb95370d19

passions empowers us to make a lasting impact, even amid challenges and doubts.

- **Age as a Number, Not a Limitation: Embracing New Beginnings**
  The author's journey back into elementary education at an older age taught him that age is merely a number, not a limitation. When we wholeheartedly pursue our dreams and aspirations, age becomes irrelevant compared to our determination, energy, and enthusiasm. Embracing new beginnings, regardless of age, allows us to live fully in alignment with our purpose. Did you know Colonel Sanders started his Kentucky Fried Chicken business when he was 62?

Reflection Questions for application:

1. **When have you experienced moments of uncertainty and felt adrift? How did you navigate those times?**
   - Consider times when you've faced crossroads and questioned your life's direction. What strategies did you use to find clarity and purpose in those moments?
2. **Who are the people in your life who have acted as beacons of wisdom and timely companionship? How have they impacted your journey?**
   - Reflect on individuals who have provided guidance and insight when you needed it most. How did their presence influence your decisions and shape your path? Is there someone who needs your encouragement and belief?
3. What unique passions and qualities do you possess that set you apart from others? How can you embrace these attributes to make a meaningful impact?

26

Distant Hearts Become United Souls: A Love Story Written By God (Part 1)

"God Blessed The Broken Roads That Led Me Straight To You"

Anticipation and excitement were high as memories of the elementary school environment flooded back. The halls were always filled with the subtle aroma of chalk dust, the faint smell of pencil shavings, glue, and paper, and the scent of fresh-baked bread rolls from the lunchroom—a reminder of the enjoyment of the learning quest, a delightful medley of childhood scents.

The vibrant scene unfolded with the sounds of children's voices, engaged in animated discussions and curious questions. Laughter danced in the air, particularly when a mischievous boy unleashed a pocket-confined frog, creating chaos and a stampede in the classroom.

These sights, sounds, and fragrances are not mere descriptions but an immersive remembrance that ignited my senses, and my heart soared with enthusiasm. Each element created a place where learning and joy intertwined in harmony.

The eve of the first day of school drew near, and a mix of apprehension and eagerness swirled within me. Seven years had passed since I was an elementary physical education teacher, since I had been teaching at a university for those years.

The concern was that my skills had grown rusty to the point of resembling an old farm tractor, battered by the sun and weather, sitting neglected in a field for a century.

The bell rang, and the children streamed into the gymnasium. Laughter and joy echoed in the air—a familiar sound that sparked my memory. As I stood before the youngins again, I was as nervous as a long-tailed cat in a room full of rocking chairs.

The room came alive with the energetic hum of youthful excitement. The giggles and a sound that resembled a cattle stampede became brushstrokes that painted a vivid scene. The energy washed over me like a gentle wave, thawing the chill of uncertainty that had settled in my heart. In that moment, surrounded by the vitality of the eager learners, I rediscovered the essence of my chosen path in education.

With certainty, I knew that I was right where I belonged, confident that the dear Lord had created this path for me.

Purpose enveloped me as I guided young minds through the labyrinth of life- skills, and choices, transcending the mere delivery of academics. I taught integrated lessons about bones, muscles, healthy eating, positive friendships, self-management, social skills, teamwork, and fitness concepts.

Primary kids are like little sponges for learning—a teacher's dream—and I reveled in the thrill of sharing knowledge with the next generation. As time progressed, colleagues became more than just coworkers; they became friends and confidants.

As I nestled into my childhood hometown, I was reminded of the quaint little village of Mayberry from the Andy Griffith show. The streets were lined with old-fashioned Victorian houses, and their architecture stood as time-honored storytellers. Front porch swings swayed, inviting a nostalgic connection to the past. The yards were well-kept and adorned with bursts of color. The turf crunched beneath my shoes, releasing the earthy scent of fresh-cut grass. Birdhouses adorned the landscapes. The presence of these little

Sparrows and Robins added a sweet melody of chirps that harmonized with the rustle of leaves.

The decision to purchase a home became a symbolic anchor, a tangible commitment to a new life and ambition. On the first day of moving in, the creak of the front door echoed a promise of new beginnings. In this idyllic setting, a new neighbor appeared with a warm welcome and a cheery smile.

"Good morning, friend! My name is Mike. My family and I live just across the street."

"Howdy! My name is Mark; pleased to meet ya!"

"Congratulations on your new home, and welcome to the neighborhood!"

"Thank you, Mike. This is a fresh start for me."

Mike handed me a plate of fresh-baked cookies, straight from the oven. More neighbors emerged like characters from a familiar story. The friendliness and helpfulness of these kind folks was like a warm embrace, and the scent of more fresh-baked goods drifted through open windows. Nostalgia embraced me as I settled into my home and this cozy neighborhood.

Three years passed, life was comfortable, and I found fulfillment in my new life. However, as we fast forward to the year 2018, it becomes apparent how the Lord blindsided me with another twist of fate, altering the course of my life.

The last breakup left me determined to remain unmarried, drawing inspiration from the Apostle Paul's example.

Relationships and dating were far from my thoughts; for my heart was invested in my relationship with God, my career, and my faithful furry companion, Marley.

One evening, as I scrolled through Facebook, connecting with my kids and grandkids, a familiar name and face caught my attention—Mai-Britt, a Norwegian foreign exchange student from my high school 40 years prior.

My memories of her are vivid. She was cuter than a box full of puppies and had stolen the hearts of about 300 boys in our school, including mine. Mai-Britt was a vibrant gymnast with boundless energy, charm, and a body to boot.

Her pictures painted a life of joyfulness, her infectious smile and vibrant personality jumping out of the pixels. The crystal blue of her eyes sparkled in every photo, and her blonde hair resembled cornsilk kissed by the sun, and framed a face that carried the years with grace.

In high school, against my heart's desire, I didn't ask her out because I was aware that she would return to Norway at the end of the year. Yet, here she was, full of life and adventure and still the embodiment of all I remembered.

To further describe her, I will use the seven S's: Sweet, Smiley, Smart, Silly, Sporty, Sexy, and Sassy. The sensory experience of my remembrance of her was like the taste of a rich blend of flavors, each characteristic leaving a distinct impression.

"Wow! This woman is so unique and incredible," I thought with a wistful smile. Fueled by curiosity and the desire to reconnect, I sent her a message. "Hey Mai-Britt, this is Mark Bruton. Do you remember me?" I typed with a sense of anticipation.

To my astonishment, she responded, "Yes, of course, I remember you! You were a bodybuilder with a kind heart and were very funny."

Those words were a melody, each carrying the rhythm of reminiscence. After divulging my hidden crush, she said, "I would have been glad to go out with you!"

All of a sudden, my emotions were like that of an old prospector who had searched all of his life for gold and, at last, found it.

Virtual interactions on Facetime became a daily occurrence and brought us closer. The screen was filled with the sight of her gorgeous smile and the sound of laughter that overflowed from our daily conversations.

"Your humor hasn't changed a bit," she said with a fond smile.

As time unfolded, I sought divine guidance through prayer. "Heavenly Father, is this the path You have set for me? Lord, I am content to embrace a single life, but this unique connection with Mai-Britt has a magnetic pull—an undeniable force like the moon tugging at the tides of my heart."

Virtual calls soon turned into real-life visits as she crossed the ocean to America for a ten-day stay—more about that in the next chapter.

During that first year, after Mai-Britt's initial visit, I also journeyed across the Atlantic Ocean to Norway five times to be with her.

Mai-Britt and I discovered that we had combined interests; we both love to cook, hike, and adventure, and we both love animals. These commonalities bonded us and filled our days with laughter and happiness.

One of my greatest privileges was getting to know her unique and remarkable family. Each personality is like a colorful bouquet of various flowers, with the Matriarch in the center as the most vibrant and scentful one. To this day, when I walk into her home, the environment always gives me a hug.

The warm scent of fresh-baked goods always lingers through the cozy kitchen and mingles with the faint aroma of spring flowers drifting in from the open window. A soft, golden glow from the sunset baths the room, casting playful shadows on the walls as it displays the ambiance and comfort of a Grandma's house.

Mai-Britt's mother, in her mid-eighties, can still outwork all of us, and her competitive spirit in family games is unmatched. She always wins, no matter what the activity is.

"Another round of cards, anyone?" comes the challenge with an ornery smile, eyebrows askew as her countenance twinkles with mischief.

A deep reflection swept over me as I pondered my new life, surrounded by Mai-Britt's loved ones; this realization dawned on me: I was not just an observer but a participant in this incredible family.

This time together was more than a mere meeting; it was a passage—a crossing of thresholds into a new chapter of shared adventures and unwritten stories. It was an honor and a privilege to be accepted into their fold, and to be part of this river of laughter and life that flowed without regard for borders or barriers.

At that moment, I witnessed the depth of their bond. Their ability to savor life's simple moments and find humor and warmth in every exchange wrapped around me like a welcome embrace. After spending this quality time with them, I was touched by their genuine affection, a tenderness that now extended to me.

Mai-Britt 1979

Mark-1979

[48]

2018

Takeaways and Lessons Learned:

1. **God's Timing is Perfect:** The author's unexpected reconnection with Mai-Britt after 40 years highlights God's impeccable timing. Sometimes, the paths we take may seem

[48] Bruton, M. W. (2024). Then and Now- [Photographs]. Personal Photos 1979, 2018.
Tool, D. E. (2024). Traveling back and forth in Love [Photograph]. Online. https://chatgpt.com/c/fec5ea38-c561-46ad-ba3c-c953cce11155

random, but God has a plan that unfolds at the right moment.

2. **The Power of Prayer and Faith:** The chapter demonstrates the importance of seeking divine guidance in significant decisions. The author's prayer for clarity and direction led to a deeper connection with Mai-Britt, emphasizing the role of faith in navigating life's uncertainties.
3. **Embracing New Beginnings:** The author's journey from being content with a single life to finding love again shows the importance of being open to new beginnings. This openness allowed for a beautiful new chapter to unfold, enriching his life in unexpected ways.

Reflection Questions for Application:

1. **How Can You Trust in God's Timing?**
   - Reflect on a time when something in your life happened unexpectedly but turned out to be a blessing. How can you apply this experience to situations which may make you question God's timing?
2. **What Role Does Prayer Play in Your Decision-Making?**
   - Think about the significant decisions you've made recently. How often do you seek God's guidance through prayer before making those decisions? How might deepening your prayer life influence your future choices?
3. **Are You Open to New Beginnings?**
   - Consider areas in your life where you might resist change or new opportunities. How can you cultivate a more open and receptive attitude, trusting that God has a plan for you that may include unexpected blessings?

27

Distant Hearts Become United Souls: A Love Story Written By God (Part 2)

Courtship, Romance, and a Beautiful Sunset

As the sun set, it painted the sky in red, orange, and gold shades. Mai-Britt's plane touched down on American soil, which signified the end of her journey from Norway and the initiation of our long-awaited reunion.

In the previous chapter, I only mentioned that Mai-Britt was the first one to travel to reunite with me in person. Allow me to lead you down memory lane to that first visit.

Up until now, everything had been virtual Facetime visits. It was now time to unite face-to-face. She came for a ten-day visit and stayed at her host mom's house to reconnect.

The air was charged with expectation the week she returned to America, as if the world held its breath for our reunion.

With the meticulous care of a modern-day Casanova, I had pre-planned an outing that promised to etch this day into the fabric of our memories—a secluded expedition to a lake hidden away in the serenity of a majestic mountain.

“I could barely contain my excitement early in the first morning, at the breakfast table.

"Britty, I have prepared a special event for us today."

She squeezed my hand, and her smile lit up the room as brightly as the sun that shone above us. The excited giggle made it all worth it.

"Really! Where are we going?"

"It`s a surprise," I said with a twinkle in my eyes.

After breakfast, Old Blue, my trusty truck, stood ready in the driveway like Cinderella`s carriage. We climbed in and set off toward the distant mountains, their silhouettes a jagged line against the dawn horizon.

The hike up the mountain was a symphony of nature's tranquility. The clean, crisp air invigorated us and carried the rich scents of pine and moist earth as we trekked our way to the mountain's peak.

There, nestled in its embrace, lay a serene lake, its surface mirroring the clear blue of the sky. Mai-Britt's hand in mine was soft and warm, her eyes reflecting the excitement in my own.

As we reached the beautiful lakeside, the gentle lap of water against the shore welcomed us. The surprise was unveiled: a quaint wooden rowboat, its sides worn smooth by time and touch.

In it was a basket containing a bottle of Grand Reserva red wine, its label speaking of years of aging and waiting for this moment. Beside it, a bundle of firewood promised warmth and light when the day would surrender to dusk.

With tender care, I helped Mai-Britt into the boat; our laughter mingled with the soft rustle of leaves in the gentle breeze.

We pushed off and glided over the glassy surface. Around us, the mountain's majesty stood stoic and covered in a drapery of green and gold.

As we rowed across the lake, the oars cutting through the water with a slight splash, the world seemed to stand still. The sun began its descent, painting the sky in strokes of orange, pink, and purple, with its reflection mirrored in the water. It was as if the heavens wanted to celebrate with us as they prepared a celestial ballet.

Raising our glasses in a tender toast, the wine had the aroma and flavor of rich berries and the promise of shared tomorrows. "To us and the life ahead," Mai-Britt whispered, her voice low yet clear.

The twinkle in her eyes outshone even the reflections on the water that sparkled. This was a moment of perfection cradled in the heart of the twilight.

"Mai-Britt, you are both ends of the rainbow, Darlin," I said with a romantic flair.

"What a beautiful thing to say," she replied, with flushed cheeks.

The warmth of the fading sun caressed our skin, and the rhythmic sound of water, as it lapped against the boat's sides, played a peaceful melody.

Later, the fire crackled on the shoreline while its flames danced, creating a cozy glow. We embraced each other and listened to the beautiful silence.

After ten days of fun and adventures, the week ended, and Mai-Britt went back to Norway. The lack of her presence left us feeling severe emptiness. Time passed, and with the help of Facetime, the courtship flourished, and our affections grew stronger.

Missing each other, we felt like a puzzle missing a main piece, so Mai-Britt arranged another visit to the States.

In the soft glow of twilight, after a year of tender courtship, a whisper from God urged me to propose to her when she returned. Determined to make it unforgettable, I began to coordinate a moment that would etch our love story into the stars.

I reached out to a local movie theater, seeking their collaboration to illuminate my proposal on their grand outdoor marquee.

The theater management embraced the idea, and a day and time were set. Three days later, I invited Mai-Britt on a date to the movies, and I could hardly contain my anticipation.

The air outside the theater carried the scent of buttered popcorn, a familiar aroma that mingled with the cool evening breeze. As we crossed the street, the distant laughter of a passersby and the gentle hum of traffic filled the air. The sight of the illuminated marquee, bathed in the warm glow of the evening, caught her attention.

Her steps slowed, and she froze in her tracks. Eyes widened, mouth agape; she was mesmerized by the sight. The marquee, a canvas of light, displayed a message that would alter the course of our lives.

"Mai-Britt, will you marry me?"

Tears welled up when her eyes met the message and glistened in the ambient light. She turned towards me and found me on one knee, holding a ring I had designed for her with meticulous care. The flags of America and Norway blended seamlessly on the ring, a visual representation of our union.

At that moment, the touch of the warm pavement beneath our feet seemed to vanish as emotions swirled. The touch of the ring, now in her possession, held the promise of a shared future.

On our way home, excitement lingered as we discussed the providence of the moment. She expressed how this union would not only shape our journey but also pave the way for smoother immigration, which would intertwine our lives on both a personal and practical level.

With great haste and joy, we went to the courthouse the next day and made it legal. We agreed to have a more formal wedding later, after I got settled.

In that enchanted environment, a deep realization settled over us like a warm blanket: our love story was part of a grander design—a tale crafted by the ruler of the universe.

The lyrics to the following song echo the sentiments of our hearts: **Keeper of the Stars** was written by Dickey Lee, Karen Staley, and Danny Mayo and sung by Tracy Byrd.

It was no accident, me finding you.
Someone had a hand in it
Long before we ever knew.

Now I just can't believe you're in my life;
Heaven's smilin' down on me
As I look at you tonight.

I tip my hat to the keeper of the stars.
He sure knew what he was doin'
When he joined these two hearts.
I hold everything
When I hold you in my arms.
I've got all I'll ever need,
Thanks to the keeper of the stars.

Soft moonlight on your face, oh, how you shine;
It takes my breath away
Just to look into your eyes.
I know I don't deserve a treasure like you,
There really are no words
To show my gratitude.

I tip my hat to the keeper of the stars,
He sure knew what he was doin'
When he joined these two hearts.
I hold everything
When I hold you in my arms.
I've got all I'll ever need,
Thanks to the keeper of the stars.
It was no accident, me finding you.
Someone had a hand in it;
Long before we ever knew. [49]

---

[49] Lee, D., Staley, K., Mayo, D., & Bird, T. (1995, February 2). Keeper Of The Stars. Song Lyrics. Retrieved June 23, 2023, from https://www.songlyrics.com/tracy-byrd/the-keeper-of-the-stars-lyrics/

2018

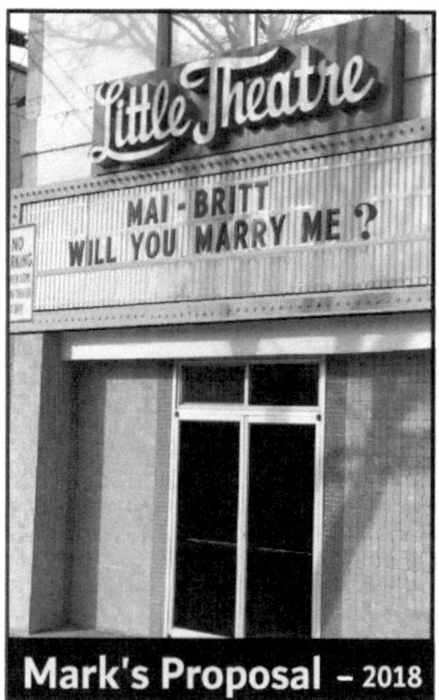

One of Mark's caricature drawings

28

Distant Hearts Become United Souls: A Love Story Written By God (Part 3)

Mai-Britt's decision to leave Norway and join me on a shared life journey in the United States weighed heavy on her heart as she was torn.

The move would require her to separate herself from the familiar comforts of home, career, and her family.

Being mindful of my three children and seven grandchildren, she thought it impossible for me to move there.

"Mark, I want to be with you, no matter where It leads, and I don't want to separate you from your loved ones," she added, her words a testament to her selflessness.

However, during my five visits to the Viking country, I witnessed the exceptional circumstances she was in with her aging parents.

Mai-Britt's house is nestled beside them, and her father's health was as fragile as a leaf in the wind.

A moment of clarity struck me while still in Norway; a sacrificial truth settled deep within my soul.

"How can I, in good conscience, uproot her from her mother and father at this critical phase of their lives?"

There was no doubt our union was part of God's plan, yet it was a sober realization when I came to terms with the fact it had to be me who made the move.

After I received this clear direction from the Lord, the decision was etched in stone. After I explained my rationale to Mai-Britt, it took a million pounds of anxiety off her shoulders.

Mai-Britt`s gratitude was heartfelt. She perceived my decision as a revelation of my true love and sacrificial commitment, a bond deeper than words.

When we shared the news with my family, a whirlwind of emotions erupted. My imminent departure caused sadness to my clan, yet all of them were thrilled by the transformative impact Mai-Britt had on my life.

The kids expressed their appreciation for the happiness she had given me.

To this day, they see her as a God-sent lifeguard in the right place at the right time who dove into the deep, dark water and pulled their father off the bottom to safety.

The selfless response of my kids was a balm to our hearts, and they reassured me by saying,

"More than anything, we want you to be happy, Dad."

My family's maturity, love, and unconditional acceptance eased the transition, though it was not without pain and adjustment.

The time grew near for me to leave my homeland and join my soulmate overseas.

The Lord had revealed His will for us to be together and for me to relocate to Norway; however, before the move could happen, we would need to sell my house.

Filled with Godfidence and the assurance that our Heavenly Father would guide us through the process as He has many times before, we were encouraged and ready for the task.

Under the vast expanse of the Colorado sky, the sun dipped below the horizon and cast shadows over the home that had sheltered me for three years. Inside, the walls echoed with prayers and memories, a testament to the life I had built on faith and solitude.

The sun descended, and a new chapter beckoned, one written by a Divine author who had penned a future far beyond the Rocky Mountains.

A supernatural strategy began as Mai-Britt planned another visit to America at a perfect time.

Now, it just so happens she has two decades of experience as a real estate agent.

Nevertheless, I still held the conviction that God would be my realtor.

"Mai-Britt, sweetheart, I want to sell my house by owner as I have always done before, and I believe God will help us."

This was a timid statement, as I did not want to offend her.

Without missing a beat, she understood my faith, took no offense, and offered support.

The quest to sell my house began with a potential buyer's interest on the first visit. Mai-Britt`s expertise in real estate proved invaluable. After a flurry of visitors, the house found its new steward in one week.

The eager buyer had been the first to cross the threshold early in the week; a young woman with a career promotion had seen beyond the empty rooms to the promise of fresh beginnings.

The woman's questions were numerous and filled with the innocence of a first-time buyer, but they were met with Mai-Britt's grace and knowledge as she weaved a seamless transition that only divine timing could orchestrate.

As we finalized the sale, the realization of leaving this part of my life behind settled in with a weight I hadn't anticipated. Mai-Britt sensed my silent contemplation and offered a smile of comfort and her support.

"It's ok, love," I reassured her, my voice steady but tinged with emotion.

"I came into this world with nothing and still have most of it."

The laughter that followed was a light in the gloom and a reminder of the joy that awaited us.

The days that came after were a whirlwind of activity. Mai-Britt had to return to Norway, and I started to sort through the remnants of my past and present.

Marley sensed the imminent change; her inquisitive gaze followed my every move. Amid the chaos, she found comfort as she would nestle down into the luggage as if to say,

"You are not going to leave me, are you?"

When the day of departure arrived, the crisp Colorado dawn was met with a resolve born of faith.

Marley and I went through the busy airport, which smelled of recycled air and sweat, as hurried passengers sprinted to their gates. We were fortunate that the smell of the food courts trumped the odor.

Marley sat tall and proud, perched on top of the suitcases as I wheeled to the flight gate. She was terrified of the escalators and would throw her little paws straight out as her eyes became as wide as coffee can lids.

After we boarded the plane, Marley jumped up into a seat and peered out the window, then gazed back at me with a perplexed and unsure grimace on her face.

The plane roared down the runway, and as it lifted off, we left behind the familiar landscape and memories, but a sense of peace enveloped me, and the Lord's presence was a constant comfort.

The future was uncertain, filled with challenges, and the task of building a new life in a foreign land. Yet, the conviction, "The Lord will provide," reverberated in my mind, a mantra that led me to this moment.

Mai-Britt awaited us at the airport in Norway, her face and smile a beacon in the crowd as we navigated the unfamiliar terrain of our fresh start.

"Welcome to your new home, my love," she said, eyes full of tears.

The puzzle was complete at last. Hand in hand, we stepped forward, not only into a marriage but also into a shared journey of faith, love, and the belief that together, with God as our guide, we would navigate the uncertain paths ahead.

The adventure was not merely a change of location but a testament to the power of divine will, a leap into the unknown with the certainty that we were where we were meant to be and would, therefore, face the future with Godfidence.

Marley traveling through the NY airport

Norway, here we come; I trust you Lord!

Photos of our Norwegian cottage tucked into the forest

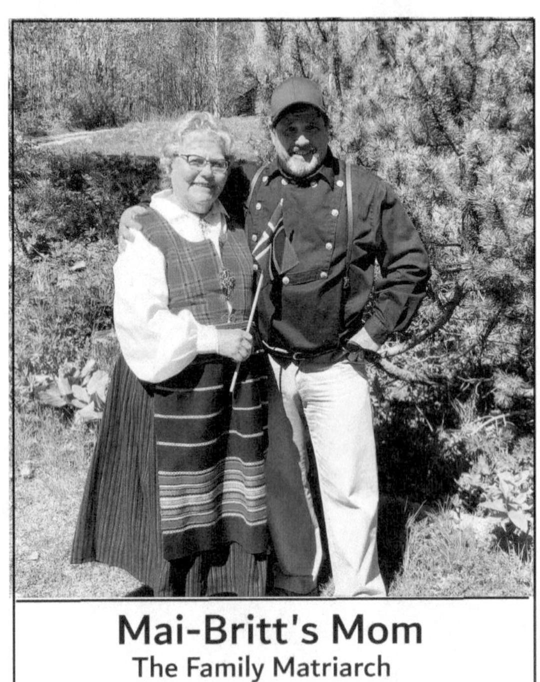

Mai-Britt's Mom
The Family Matriarch

Takeaways and lessons learned.

1. **Selfless Love and Sacrifice:** This chapter highlights the profound nature of selfless love and the sacrifices it often entails. The author's decision to move to Norway instead of asking Mai-Britt to leave her ailing parents is a testament to the depth of his commitment and love.
2. **Faith in Divine Guidance:** The narrative demonstrates a strong reliance on faith and divine guidance in making life-altering decisions. The central themes are the author's belief that their union is part of God's plan and his confidence in God's provision throughout the process.
3. **Family Support and Acceptance:** The chapter underscores the importance of family support and acceptance during significant life transitions. The author's family, despite their sadness, shows maturity and unconditional love by

supporting his decision and recognizing the positive impact Mai-Britt has had on his life.

Reflection Questions for Application:

1. **How Can I Demonstrate Selfless Love in My Relationships?**
   - Reflect on how you can show selfless love and make sacrifices for the well-being and happiness of your loved ones. Consider moments when you might have put your own needs aside for the benefit of someone else
2. **In What Ways Has Faith Guided My Major Life Decisions?**
   - Think about significant decisions in your life and how faith or a sense of divine guidance played a role. How did trusting in something greater than yourself shape your outcomes and sense of peace during those times?
3. **How Do I Support and Accept My Loved Ones' Choices?**
   - Consider how you react to the major decisions of those you care about. Reflect on instances where you have provided support and acceptance, even when those decisions may have been difficult for you. How can you continue to offer unconditional love and encouragement?

29

Trust in the Unknown: From Relocation to Vocation

An Extraordinary Tale of Faith, Employment Challenges, and Divine Blessings

"Are you kidding me, Bruton? You are moving to another country without a job lined up? Were you dropped on your head when you were little?" Questioned many of my friends before I left America for Norway. "You know, Mark, wisdom has been chasing you, but you have always been faster. This one takes the cake!"

Trying to explain how God works doesn't always make sense. Therefore, I decided to let them watch how He would work this out and why I walk in Godfidence.

Relocating to a foreign country is a logistical maze involving various bureaucratic steps. Obtaining a new social security number and a bank account is necessary even for non-citizens. The process, however, becomes more complex when you need a job to make it all come together. The immovable object meets an unstoppable force, so to speak.

The enormity of this transition was compounded by my 5,000-mile journey across the ocean, driven by faith, to be with my soulmate and love of my life. Trusting in God's orchestration, I believed He held the reins over the circumstances.

During one of my visits to Norway, I learned about an IB International School that taught all subjects in English. This was significant, given my limited grasp of the local language. Learning Norwegian is challenging, and finding work without fluency seemed almost impossible. Discovering an English-speaking institution was a remarkable stroke of good fortune and blessing. Seeing an opportunity, I decided to introduce myself.

"Greetings," I said to the head administrator, extending my hand with a firm grip and a confident smile. "My name is Mark Bruton, and I've been told wonderful things about your IB school. I am highly interested in joining your team as a teacher."

After meeting with the principal, I submitted my resume–or CV as they refer to it in Europe–and toured the quaint campus and facilities, catching a glimpse of the expansive handball arena that served as the gymnasium for the physical education program. However, no openings were available then, and after the initial interaction, there was no further correspondence for the rest of the year. Therefore, I assumed this wasn't part of God's plan, even though I didn't comprehend its reasons. Yet, the Lord reminded me not to rely on my own understanding (Proverbs 3:5-6).

One year later, after relocating to Norway, I heeded the advice of Mai-Britt's mom and decided to reintroduce myself to the head administrator.

"Hello again, Mr. Armano," I said with a smile. "As you will recall, we met last October, and I wanted to let you know that I am now married and residing here in Gjøvik. You should know that I am very interested in substitute teaching or any available employment."

The principal was cheerful and inviting, appreciating the update, but no immediate openings were discussed. He was a man who played his cards close to his vest.

However, that same weekend, while visiting friends in a distant town, I received an email from the administrator. He stated that a

PYP primary physical education role had just opened—a half-time job.

A prompt reply was in order. "Dear, Mr. Armano, I am thrilled to accept the PYP Health and Physical Education position you have offered. Thank you for this opportunity."

This was only my first week in Norway, and we were excited and full of praise for this new open door. This IB educational institution comprises students and staff from around the world. It is an international hub that presented a unique educational concept for me to embrace—the International Baccalaureate (IB). My devotion to my wife superseded any challenge, and I was determined to learn and adapt.

During my initial week, the head of the school also inquired about my willingness to teach MYP Digital Design. MYP is Seventh through tenth grade. Although unfamiliar with the subject and out of my wheelhouse, I pledged to learn and instruct any subject they needed and obtain the necessary training to be certified.

I assured Mr. Armano, "I am more than willing to do whatever it takes to contribute to the school and students' success." Though grateful, inside, I was as nervous as a rabbit at a coyote convention.

These expanded responsibilities brought me almost to full-time hours, and the compensation was much higher than I had ever experienced in the United States.

We were off to a miraculous start, except for one major hitch. When moving to another country, especially in Norway, obtaining employment or accepting a contract requires UDI approval, a concept akin to American immigration or a green card work visa. However, this process resembled an insurmountable river to navigate.

One had to secure this approval before employment could be guaranteed—a task that could span up to six months for the permission to materialize. The contract being offered to me was to begin in two weeks. Despite the daunting nature of this challenge, I held to my faith that my Heavenly Father was the God of the impossible.

"Dear Lord, we need your help." This was our plea as we approached the police station to submit a stack of documents comprising what looked like a million pages and $1,200.

The Lord answered and intervened when Mai-Britt crossed paths with an old high school friend as we entered the building. The two of them had a joyous conversation, laughing and reminiscing about days gone by. Oh, did I mention that she just happened to be the person in charge of the RUDI legal immigration papers?

My precious wife had spent meticulous hours ensuring all the forms were organized and aligned with the required format.

Expressing our gratitude, we said, "Thank you so much for your help; we appreciate your assistance." The lady conveyed her intent to expedite the massive packet to the powers that be.

Acknowledging my job offer from the school, she vowed to do her utmost to accelerate the process, but made it clear that she could not promise anything.

Here is where the miracle unfolds. The contract from the school couldn't be signed without the UDI approval. With her assurance to communicate by the following week, we left trusting God. This encounter unfolded on a Wednesday.

As I washed dishes the next day, I said: "Lord, it would be nothing for You to hasten this process. Can you please have them call today or at least by Friday?"

Remarkably, as I had hoped and prayed, my wife received a call from her friend at the RUDI.

A joyful voice was on the line: "Hello, Mai-Britt. We are ready for Mark to come down, retrieve his documents, provide fingerprints and a photograph, and we will get this process moving."

This quick approval allowed me to open a bank account and accept employment within hours. The school's office manager was dumbfounded by how quickly I had been approved.

"Mark, we are so impressed by how fast everything came together; we have never seen anyone obtain approval so soon!" This, of course, allowed me to brag about my Heavenly Father and His goodness.

Once again, the Lord had showcased His faithfulness in a rapid turn of events. This experience solidified my understanding of how God had orchestrated my decision to be with Mai-Britt and relocate to Norway. Her family became my own, and I enjoyed a sense of belonging I had never experienced before.

In gratefulness, I have come to cherish her family. Her mother, a source of inspiration and a true matriarch, and her father, a true embodiment of strength, character, and hard work, left an indelible mark on me.

When her father passed away, I thanked God that I was present to support my love during her time of mourning. We said goodbye to him, which was heart-wrenching, but thanked the dear Lord. My presence gave solace during her time of need.

Over the past five years, our bond has deepened. We live in a charming little cottage tucked away in the dense Norwegian forest, overlooking a magnificent lake. Contentment permeates our existence. Oh, the fulfillment of experiencing such profound happiness!

Because we live in Europe, we have been blessed to travel the world together. It has been a blessing to tour countries like Ireland, Spain, France, Germany, and Sweden, and Lord willing, there are many more to come.

In the summers, we also enjoy visiting the States to spend time with our kids and grandkids. We dream of spending half the year in Colorado and half in Norway. Prayers are already at work for this to come to fruition.

Our spiritual growth continues in parallel with our life journey. Now, I am immersed in my role as a passionate educator, and Mai-Britt is fulfilled and enjoying her Massage Therapy business.

As our story unfolds, I will return to my legacy book to add more chapters as life evolves. Until the Lord calls me home, I remain devoted to sharing the testament of God's extraordinary workings in my life. My faith is rooted in trusting Jesus, who sacrificed his life for us all.

In closing this final chapter, I want to dedicate the words of a powerful song to my precious wife and give God the glory for all he has done in our lives. The music is performed by Rascal Flatts and co-written by Jeff Hanna and Markus Hummon. It tells our love story perfectly and the divine hand behind it all.

(*Song Lyrics:* ***God Blessed the Broken Road - Bing,*** **n.d.**).

I set out on a narrow way many years ago,
Hoping I would find true love along the broken road.
But I got lost a time or two,
I wiped my brow and kept pushin' through.
I couldn't see how every sign pointed straight to you,
Every long-lost dream led me to where you are.
Others who broke my heart;
They were like northern stars
Pointing me on my way into your loving arms.
This much I know is true,
That God blessed the broken road
That led me straight to you.
Yes, He did!
I think about the years I spent just passin' through,
I'd like to have the time I lost and give it back to you.
But you smile and take my hand;
You've been there, you understand.
It's all part of a grander plan that is coming true.

Every long-lost dream led me to where you are.
Others who broke my heart;
They were like northern stars
Pointing me on my way into your loving arms.
This much I know is true,
That God blessed the broken road
That led me straight to you. [50]

For anyone reading this, I extend a challenge: embrace Godfidence, placing trust in God. Surrender to Jesus Christ, knowing that although you will stumble and fall, the good shepherd is perpetually present to aid you at every juncture. I hope you have found inspiration in my story and that it has drawn your heart closer to our Heavenly Father. Lord willing, I will return to share more. There's more to unfold, and as I continue my journey, I'll forever praise the wonders God has wrought in my life.

Takeaways and Lessons Learned:

Embracing Godfidence: This chapter vividly demonstrates the concept of "Godfidence"—trusting in God's plan and timing, even when circumstances seem uncertain or challenging. The author's unwavering faith in God's orchestration through significant life changes underscores the power of divine guidance and the peace that comes from relying on a higher power.

1. **The Power of Perseverance**: The journey of relocating to a new country, securing employment, and integrating into a new culture highlights the importance of perseverance.

[50] God Blessed The Broken Road By Marcus Hummon, Bobby Boyd, and Jeff Hanna. (1994, January 2). In Wikipedia. https://en.wikipedia.org/wiki/Bless_the_Broken_Road

Despite numerous obstacles, including bureaucratic hurdles and the challenge of learning a new language, the author's determination and faith carried him through.

2. **The Impact of Love and Support**: The chapter emphasizes the profound impact of love and support from family and community. The author's relationship with Mai-Britt, his acceptance into her family, and the support he received from both his own family and new acquaintances in Norway were crucial in navigating his new life.

Reflection Questions for Application:

1. **How Can I Cultivate Trust in Uncertain Times?**
   - Reflect on areas of your life where you face uncertainty. How can you cultivate a deeper trust through faith, perseverance, or seeking support from loved ones? Consider specific steps you can take to embrace the unknown with confidence and faith.
2. **What Challenges Have Strengthened My Perseverance?**
   - Think about the challenges you have faced that required significant perseverance. How did overcoming these obstacles shape your character and outlook on life? Reflect on how past experiences of perseverance can inspire you to tackle current or future challenges.
3. **How Do I Show Love and Support to Those Around Me?**
   - Consider how you demonstrate love and support to the important people in your life. How can you be more intentional in offering your encouragement and assistance during their times of need? Reflect on how you can create a supportive environment for your loved ones, just as the author and his community did.

[51]

[51] Time, D. (n.d.). American and Norwegian Flags Blended into One. Dreamstime.com. Retrieved June 18, 2018, from https://thumbs.dreamstime.com/z/connected-heart-flags-norway-america-vector-heart-flags-norway-us-vector-263800450.jpg

30

How can I come to know This Amazing God?

Embrace His Love Today

Dear Reader,

As you turn to the last pages of "Godfidence," you've journeyed through stories that illustrate the awe-inspiring power and boundless love of a great God. These stories aren't just tales; they're invitations—direct and heartfelt—urging you to discover and embrace this God for yourself. Today, I want to share the most important decision you will ever make: Give your life to Jesus Christ.

Life is filled with moments that define us, but none is as crucial as choosing to accept God's gift of salvation. This decision transcends time and transforms your eternity. It's an invitation to enter a relationship with the Creator, who loves you more deeply than you can imagine.

Your Path to Salvation

- **Recognize Your Need for Salvation**
    - **Romans 3:23** - "For all have sinned and fall short of the glory of God."
    - We've all made mistakes and strayed from God's perfect plan. This verse reminds us that everyone needs God's grace.

- **Understand the Consequences of Sin**
  - **Romans 6:23** - "For the wages of sin is death, but the gift of God is eternal life in Christ Jesus our Lord."
  - Sin leads to separation from God, but He offers us the gift of eternal life through Jesus. This gift is freely given, waiting for you to accept it.

- **Believe in God's Love for You**
  - **Romans 5:8** - "But God demonstrates His own love for us in this: While we were still sinners, Christ died for us."
  - Even in our brokenness, God's love never wavers. Jesus' sacrifice on the cross is the ultimate demonstration of His love for you.

- **Confess and Believe**
  - **Romans 10:9-10** - "If you declare with your mouth, 'Jesus is Lord,' and believe in your heart that God raised Him from the dead, you will be saved. For it is with your heart that you believe and are justified, and it is with your mouth that you profess your faith and are saved."
  - Salvation comes through faith in Jesus. It's about believing in your heart and confessing with your mouth that Jesus is Lord.

- **Receive God's Assurance**
  - **Romans 10:13** - "Everyone who calls on the name of the Lord will be saved."
  - This promise is for you. When you call on Jesus, He promises to hear and save you.
  - ***Remember, you do not have to make yourself clean to come to God; You come to God to be made clean.***

- **Jesus is THE way to Heaven**
  - **John 14:1-6 NIV -** "Do not let your hearts be troubled. You believe in God; believe also in me. My Father's house has many rooms; if that were not so, would I have told you that I am going there to prepare a place for you? And if I go and prepare a place for you, I will come back and take you to be with me that you also may be where I am. You know the way to the place where I am going."

Thomas said to him, "Lord, we don't know where you are going, so how can we know the way?"

Jesus answered, "I am the way and **the truth** and **the life. No one comes to the Father except through me.**

John 3:16 NIV

In the following verse, replace the words world and whoever with your name.

16. For God so loved the world that he gave his one and only Son, that whoever believes in him shall not perish but have eternal life.

Make the Decision Today

Dear friend, don't let this moment pass you by. God's love is reaching out to you right now, inviting you into a life of purpose, peace, and eternal joy. You don't have to be perfect; you can come as you are and accept His grace.

If you are ready to take this step, pray this sincere prayer:

"Dear God, I come to You in prayer, confessing that I am a sinner. I believe that Jesus Christ is Your Son, who died for my sins and rose from the dead. I ask for Your forgiveness. I turn away from my sins and invite Jesus into my heart and life. I want to trust Him as my Savior and follow Him as my Lord. Thank You for Your grace and for giving me the gift of eternal life. In Jesus' name, I pray. Amen."

If you've said that prayer, I want to extend my heartfelt congratulations on your life-altering decision to surrender to Christ! This act of asking Jesus to take the reins of your life is not just significant; it's transformative. It's the most pivotal decision you will ever make.

As you embark on this new journey of faith, finding a solid Bible-based church is paramount. It's a place where you can be enveloped by a community of believers who will support, encourage, and guide you. Make it a priority to start reading the Bible daily; it's not just a book, it's God's Word, your guide, your strength, and your source of wisdom as you nurture your relationship with Him.

Furthermore, seek out a mature individual in their faith to mentor you, someone who can walk beside you, answer your questions and help you navigate this new chapter in your life. Remember, spiritual growth is a journey that requires intentional steps—be diligent in prayer, immerse yourself in Scripture, and commit to fellowship with other believers. Now is the time to lay a strong foundation that will sustain you for a lifetime. Don't delay—every step you take in faith brings you closer to the fullness of life that God has for you.

[52]

"Come to me, all you who are weary and burdened, and I will give you rest. Take my yoke upon you and learn from me, for I am gentle and humble in heart, and you will find rest for your souls. For my yoke is easy, and my burden is light." **Mathew 11: 28-30**

Not The End;
the journey continues.

[52] TOOL, D. E. (2024). *Jesus Welcomes You* [Digital image]. Online. https://chatgpt.com/c/93ab4135-5a6c-497f-a0d9-39f7e5267ac6

References

Introduction: Tool, D. E. (2024). *Good Versus Evil* [Photograph]. Online. https://chatgpt.com/c/5f5217cb-e104-4e80-82b0-8c842be4e86a

Divine Whispers: Tool., D. E. (2024). *Open Bible radiating light* [Photograph]. Online. https://chatgpt.com/c/bec1e8aa-0a5c-4a6b-954c-dda331a0abcd

Chapter 1:

- Tool, D. E. (2024). Little Boy Defending His Mother [Digital image]. Online.OpenAI. (2024). ChatGPT (4o) [Large language model]. https://chatgpt.com/c/67956650-b0da-4db0-a561-08825e073d46

Chapter 2:

- Carmichael, R. (1958). The Savior is Waiting (p. online). https://thescottspot.wordpress.com/2016/09/21/the-savior-is-waiting-written-in-1958/

- Tool, D. E. (2024). Final Surrender [Digital image]. Online.Tool, D. E. (2024). Young Man Asking God for Help [Digital image]. Online.OpenAI. (2024). ChatGPT (4o) [Large language model]. https://chatgpt.com/c/67956650-b0da-4db0-a561-08825e073d46

Chapter 3:

- Adrianisms: Rogers, A. (2006). Online: Adrianisms (p. Quotations). Love Worth Finding. https://www.lwf.org/adrianisms

- Bruton, M. W., Tool, D. E. (2024). When Baptism Goes Awry [Digital Art]. Online. OpenAI. (2024). ChatGPT (4o) [Large language model]. https://chatgpt.com/c/67956650-b0da-4db0-a561-08825e073d46

Chapter 4:

- Crouch, A. (n.d.). Through it All. Zion Lyrics. Retrieved February 25, 2023, from https://zionlyrics.com/lyrics/andrae-crouch-through-it-all-ive-learned-to-trust-in-jesus-lyricsae

- Blake, W. (n.d.). *On Another's Sorrow.* Poem Analysis. Retrieved August 21, 2024, from https://poemanalysis.com/william-blake/on-anothers-sorrow/

- Tool, D. E. (2024). Saying Goodbye to Dad [Digital image]. Online. OpenAI. (2024). ChatGPT (4o) [Large language model]. https://chatgpt.com/c/67956650-b0da-4db0-a561-08825e073d46

Chapter 5:

- Bruton, M. W. Tool, D. E. (2024). Brother Bill Reading the Word [Photograph]. Online. OpenAI. (2024). ChatGPT (4o) [Large language model].

https://chatgpt.com/c/1cb7f7ec-6b42-4603-a436-2f25698f6653

Chapter 6:

- Randle, L., & Dartt, T. (n.d.). *God On the Mountain.* Genius. Retrieved August 21, 2024, from https://genius.com/Lynda-randle-god-on-the-mountain-lyrics/q/writer

- Cowman, L. (2008). Poem, Rain, Rain (3rd ed.). Zondervan. (2008). Streams in The Desert (3rd ed.). Zondervan. https://www.amazon.com/s?i=stripbooks&rh=p_27%3AL.+B.+E.+Cowman&s=relevancerank&text=L.+B.+E.+Cowman&ref=dp_byline_sr_book_1

- Hamilton, R. B. (2023). I walked a mile with Pleasure (1st ed.). Good Reads-Online. https://www.goodreads.com/quotes/289683-i-walked-a-mile-with-pleasure-she-chatted-all-the

- McEntire, R. (2008, February 1). *If I had only known.* LYRICS. Retrieved August 8, 2023, from https://www.lyrics.com/lyric/30201544/Reba+McEntire/If+I+Had+Only+Known#google_vignette

- Tool, D. E. (2024). Depiction of Vandi [Photograph]. Online. OpenAI. (2024). ChatGPT (4o) [Large language model]. https://chatgpt.com/c/67956650-b0da-4db0-a561-08825e073d46'

- Tool, D. E. (2024). My Brothers Rodeo Accident- "Last Ride" [Digital image]. ONLINE. OpenAI. (2024).

ChatGPT (4o) [Large language model]. https://chatgpt.com/c/b7dd579d-77b0-4696-91c7-0eb99978233e3

- Tool, D. E. (2024). University Of Adversity [Digital image]. ONLINE. OpenAI. (2024). ChatGPT (4o) [Large language model]. https://chatgpt.com/c/30da19ab-5766-489c-8989-31f7f5ae831b

- Tool, D. E. (2024). Vandi Goes Home To Heaven [Digital image]. Online. OpenAI. (2024). ChatGPT (4o) [Large language model]. https://chatgpt.com/c/67956650-b0da-4db0-a561-08825e073d46

Chapter 7:

Tool, D. E. (2024). *Doctor Jesus* [Digital depiction]. Online. https://chatgpt.com/c/93ab4135-5a6c-497f-a0d9-39f7e5267ac6

Chapter 8:

- Bruton, M. W. (2024). Homes: Answer To Prayer [Photograph]. Personal Photos.

Chapter 9:

- Tool, D. E. (2024). Keystone Comedy Team- Painting the Church Steeple [Photograph]. Online. OpenAI. (2024). ChatGPT (4o) [Large language model]. https://chatgpt.com/c/f6aafc73-2866-4a1c-b125-8d524968f22e?model=gpt-4o

Chapter 10:

- Tool, D. E. (2024). Mark Proposes to Ann [Digital Image]. Online. OpenAI. (2024). ChatGPT (4o) [Large language model]. https://chatgpt.com/c/6e9f9c59-5844-47e1-956b-7a3b43bb83ff

- Tool, D. E. (2024). Match Makers: The Valentines Banquet [Digital image]. Online. OpenAI. (2024). ChatGPT (4o) [Large language model]. https://chatgpt.com/c/b7dd579d-77b0-4696-91c7-0eb9978233e3

Chapter 11:

- Tool, D. E. (2024). Mark and Ann buy their first home [Digital image]. Online. OpenAI. (2024). ChatGPT (4o) [Large language model]. https://chatgpt.com/c/b7dd579d-77b0-4696-91c7-0eb9978233e3

- Tool, D. E. (2024). Mark and Ann with quintuplets [Digital image]. Online. OpenAI. (2024). ChatGPT (4o) [Large language model]. https://chatgpt.com/c/b7dd579d-77b0-4696-91c7-0eb9978233e3

Chapter 12:

- Tool, D. E. (2024). ChatGPT (4o) [Large language model]. https://chatgpt.com/c/b7dd579d-77b0-4696-91c7-0eb9978233e3

Chapter 13:

- Bruton, M. W. (2024). Little Tykes Playset [Photograph]. Personal Photos.

Chapter 14:

- Bruton, M. W. (2024). Farm Life [Photograph]. Personal Photos.

Chapter 15:

- Bruton, M. W. (2024). Blue Astro Van- Digitally Enhanced [Photograph]. Personal Photos.

Chapter 16:

- Tool, D. E. (2024). Calf In The Van [Digital depiction]. Online. https://chatgpt.com/c/a9d97728-b6ef-4edd-b1e2-02dbe9a44e01

Chapter 17:

- Cowman, L. B. E., & Reimann, J. (1958, August 15). Poem: "Oh Thou Of Little Faith". Christianity.com. Retrieved June 29, 2023, from https://www.christianity.com/devotionals/streams-in-the-desert/
- Tool, D. E. (2023). Victor Payback [Digital depiction]. Online. https://chatgpt.com/c/6988419c-9a75-4319-bb82-6a2adfea6df5

Chapter 18:

- Tool, D. E. (2024). The Baird Brothers [Digital depiction]. Online. https://chatgpt.com/c/9a047a65-b009-4492-bb90-d8e49dd59e32

- Cowman, L. (2024, August 1). August First. Streams in the Desert. Retrieved August 1, 2024, from Cowman, L. B. E.; Reimann, Jim. Zondervan. Kindle Edition.

Chapter 19:

Tool, D. E. (2023). *Return to teaching* [Photograph]. Online. https://chatgpt.com/c/dd8ca2ba-5dd1-4cfa-aa20-1c7b987fe4bb

- Marcelina, M. (2017). Analisis Lindung Nilai (Hedging) Pada Perusahaan Badan Usaha Milik. https://core.ac.uk/download/540177655.pdf

- Streams in the Desert - Cowman, L. (2024, August 1). August First. Streams in the Desert. Retrieved August 1, 2024, from Cowman, L. B. E.; Reimann, Jim. Zondervan. Kindle Edition.

- Tool, D. E. (2024). Mark teaching physical education [Digital image depiction]. Online. OpenAI. (2024). ChatGPT (4o) [Large language model]. https://chatgpt.com/c/b7dd579d-77b0-4696-91c7-0eb9978233e3

Chapter 20:

- Anonymous, A. (n.d.). Two Natures at War. Goodreads. Retrieved June 15, 2023, from https://www.goodreads.com/quotes/507804-two-natures-beat-within-my-breast-the-one-is-foul?fbclid=IwY2xjawEa3JlleHRuA2FlbQIxMAABHXNs6yHY_sHVNi_6tqhSdytbY3CVVn51585qOaiVrLoD4TLm5ggQDWp8A_aem_uKoZjuSTzCAjtHZM8hyfkQ

- Faith That Moves God - Hudson, K. (2018, August 18). Faith That Moves God. Sermons by Logos. Retrieved June 15, 2024, from https://sermons.logos.com/sermons/346119-faith-that-move-god?sso=false

- Galatians 6:1 - Version, Y. (n.d.). Galatians 6:1. You Version Online Bible. Retrieved July 26, 2024, from https://www.bible.com/bible/116/gal.6.1.NLT

- Krishna, R. (2023, November 9). A Journey of Hope: Battling the Tumor. Mango Health. Retrieved June 27, 2023, from https://mangohealth.org/2023/11/09/a-journey-of-hope-battling-the-tumor/

- Love Without End Amen - Aaron Barker / George Straight (n.d.). Love Without End, Amen. Letras. Retrieved June 21, 2023, from https://www.letras.mus.br/george-strait/38696/#google_vignette

- Sad Couple growing apart - Tool, E. E. (2024). Sad couple growing apart [Photograph]. Online. https://chatgpt.com/c/69ff991c-b68f-4c48-945d-bd424097bb6b

- Trammell, M. (2010, January 5). Sin Will Take You Farther. Flashlyrics. Retrieved June 19, 2024, from https://www.flashlyrics.com/lyrics/the-cathedrals/sin-will-take-you-farther-39

Chapter 21:

- Bruton, M. W. (2024). New Kansas Home. Dodge City, Kansas- [Photograph]. Personal Photos 2000.

Chapter 22:

- TOOL, D. E. (2024, June 25). Pushing Through and Moving Forward. Chat GPT 4.0. Retrieved June 25, 2024, from https://chatgpt.com/c/ba895eaf-f18e-4ea7-aea7-3a169f6d581f

- Tool, E. E. (2024, July 28). Mark's Transparency With Cindy. Chat GPT 4.0. Retrieved July 28, 2024, from https://chatgpt.com/c/2df683d1-66f3-41a7-9070-85070b7f8481

Chapter 23:

- Goke, D., Phillips, R., Herms, B., & West, M. (2014, January 5). About Tell Your Heart to Beat Again. Lyrics. Retrieved June 24, 2023, from https://www.lyrics.com/lyric/30872913/Tell+Your+Heart+to+Beat+Again

- RED UP (n.d.). Why Boring Everyday Tasks Are Actually Good for You: Embracing Routine, Developing Life Skills, and Finding Joy in the Mundane. RED AI. Retrieved June 8, 2024, from https://marketingbyred.com/marketing/why-boring-everyday-tasks-are-actually-good-for-you-embracing-routine-developing-life-skills-and-finding-joy-in-the-mundane/

Chapter 24:

- Cowman, L. (2008). Poem: They On The Heights. Streams in The Desert. Zondervan. https://www.christianity.com/devotionals/streams-in-the-desert/

- TOOL, D. E. (2024). Bible Characters Who Failed but Were Used by God [Digital depiction]. Online. https://chatgpt.com/c/10410378-2528-4ae0-be6e-61a2e6563765

Chapter 25:

- Tool, D. E. (2024). Interview and Job Offer [Digital depiction]. Online. https://chatgpt.com/c/175b167a-c53b-451b-a539-3adb95370d19

Chapter 26:

- Bruton, M. W. (2024). Then and Now- [Photographs]. Personal Photos 1979, 2018.

- Tool, D. E. (2024). Traveling back and forth in Love [Photograph]. Online. https://chatgpt.com/c/fec5ea38-c561-46ad-ba3c-c953cce11155

Chapter 27:

- Bruton, M. W. (2024). Mark and Mai-Britt reunite after 40 yrs. [Photograph]. Personal Photos 2018.

- Lee, D., Staley, K., Mayo, D., & Bird, T. (1995, February 2). Keeper Of The Stars. Song Lyrics. Retrieved June 23,

2023, from https://www.songlyrics.com/tracy-byrd/the-keeper-of-the-stars-lyrics/

Chapter 28:

➢ Bruton, M. W. (2024). Mark and Marley Move To Norway [Photograph]. Personal Photos 2019.

Chapter 29:

➢ God Blessed The Broken Road By Marcus Hummon, Bobby Boyd, and Jeff Hanna. (1994, January 2). In Wikipedia. https://en.wikipedia.org/wiki/Bless_the_Broken_Road

➢ Time, D. (n.d.). American and Norwegian Flags Blended into One. Dreamstime.com. Retrieved June 18, 2018, from https://thumbs.dreamstime.com/z/connected-heart-flags-norway-america-vector-heart-flags-norway-us-vector-263800450.jpg

Chapter 30:

➢ TOOL, D. E. (2024). *Jesus Welcomes You* [Digital image]. Online. https://chatgpt.com/c/93ab4135-5a6c-497f-a0d9-39f7e5267ac6

About the Author

Mark Bruton is a devoted Christian husband, father, and grandfather who shares his faith through powerful storytelling. His life experiences and unwavering commitment to education shape his heartfelt narratives, inspiring readers to understand God's love and grace in a much deeper way.

Mark's academic journey is a testament to his commitment to education and faith. He holds a BA in teaching from Mesa State Colorado University and studied pastoral studies at Intermountain Bible College. He also earned a master's degree in administration from the University of Northern Colorado. Mark has profoundly impacted countless lives with over eighteen years as a pastor and 32 years as a teacher and coach.

He served as an adjunct professor at Western Colorado University for seven years, mentoring students and leaving a lasting impact. Mark currently lives in Norway with his Norwegian wife, Mai-Britt, and their two dogs, Marley and Balder. He teaches at an IB International School and embraces diverse cultures from around the world.

Mark is renowned for his ability to infuse everyday life with faith, drawing from his personal experiences with miraculous answers to prayer and divine encounters. His writing style is both thought-provoking and amusing. Mark is a master of using one-liners and colloquialisms that will leave you either soul-searching or belly-laughing.

Mark's love for nature reflects his faith and creativity. An avid outdoorsman, he enjoys hiking, fishing, and exploring the beauty of the natural world. His creative talents extend to freelance artistry, producing commissioned works worldwide. Mark's debut book, *Godfidence*, is evidence of his faith and gratitude. This book is a legacy for his children and seven grandchildren and also to encourage life's weary travelers who may find its pages.

Mark's unique blend of real-life anecdotes and profound spiritual insights resonates with readers. It deeply impacts them, creating a sense of community and shared experience and offering renewed hope and inspiration. He does not write for the perfect Christians but rather for those who, like him, have experienced struggles and setbacks in their faith journey, what he fondly refers to as the 'Broken Halo Club '.

Mark's experiences will inspire you to embrace your own faith journey and ignite a newfound trust in the God who turns trauma, depression, anxiety, guilt, fear, rejection, failure, and doubt into confidence in His ability to change things for your good. As you read, we are confident that God will become more real to you than ever, filling you with hope and reassurance. Dive into "Godfidence" and find out for yourself.

Made in the USA
Columbia, SC
05 October 2024